M000289882

# unstuck

## BY RICH MILLER

unstuck
Eight discipleship studies to help you experience freedom in Christ

Published by Freedom in Christ Ministries
9051 Executive Park Dr. Suite 503
Knoxville, TN 37923

www.ficm.org

© 2015 by Rich Miller

All rights reserved. No part of this book may be reproduced or transmitted in any form or by any means, electronic or mechanical, including photocopying, recording or by any information storage and retrieval system, without permission of the author or publisher, except for the inclusion of brief quotation in a review or article, when credit to the book, publisher and order information are included in the review or article.

ISBN: 978-099-697-2512

Scripture Quotations
Unless otherwise indicated, Scripture quotations are taken from the
New American Standard Bible, © 1960, 1962,1963, 1971, 1972, 1973, 1975, 1977, 1995 by the Lockman Foundation. Used by permission.

The Holy Bible, New International Version®, NIV® Copyright © 1973, 1978, 1984, 2011 by Biblica, Inc.® Used by permission. All rights reserved worldwide.

The Holy Bible, English Standard Version® (ESV®)
Copyright © 2001 by Crossway, a publishing ministry of Good News Publishers.
All rights reserved.
ESV Text Edition: 2011

Cover design by
Mike Taylor, Taylor Graphix
taylorgraphix@knology.net
Knoxville, Tennessee

Cartoons and illustrations © 2015 by Mike Taylor. All rights reserved.

Book layout by
Courtney Gibson
www.courtneygibson.net

Printed in the United States

# contents

## >> Note to those using this material on your own:

You can work through the material in this book alone, if you really want to. It would be a lot better, however, to try and find at least one other person with whom you can go through these studies. You will have a lot more fun and I think you will get a lot more out of it that way. As Ecclesiastes says, "Two are better than one..." (Ecclesiastes 4:9). In light of that, you'll find my approach in writing this book assumes that two or more of you are going through it together.

## >> Note to those in discipleship relationships:

I have set up these studies to work better if you complete them ahead of time. That way the participants will have all the content read and questions answered in advance and the leader can then choose which parts to focus on during the actual meeting. Pray for those in your group each week and have fun! Don't feel that you have to cover the whole lesson in one week if you don't have time. This is designed as an eight-week study but it can easily go longer. God won't mind.

# getting unstuck

## welcome!

Whether you are a seasoned veteran of the Christian faith, a newbie or somewhere in between, welcome to this series of eight studies we call *unstuck*. What is on these pages has wrestled its way out of the crucible of my own painful struggles in life and ministry.

## my story

I first got unstuck... by the grace of God... in college when, as an arrogant, skeptical agnostic, Jesus invaded my personal space and set up shop in my life. There are no words to describe how grateful I am that He did that. After the initial rush of knowing I was really alive and forgiven in Christ, though, He began to tackle my pride and self-sufficiency. I had no idea He was going to do that, and nobody bothered to tell me. (It must have been in the fine print somewhere!) I found out later it's His plan for all of us—absolutely necessary but no fun.

Anyway, as a junior in college, I waved the white flag and surrendered to Him as my Lord. That was the second instance where I got unstuck... from being a defeated, discouraged Christian to one beginning to experience the power of God's Spirit. What a relief and change that made!

The concept of "freedom," however, didn't pop up on my radar screen until many years later. I was in full-time Christian ministry, married, with a new kid and far away from home, in the Philippines. Despite many years of seeking to follow Christ, there were still major areas of rejection, insecurity, anger, control and envy that had me... you guessed it... stuck. You would've thought I would have "got it" by that time. Well, I hadn't.

Enter "God's Unsticking Strategy #3." Discovering my freedom in Christ has enabled me to move from knowing Jesus, not only as Savior and Lord, but also as my Daily Life and Strength. And so, as I continue to learn and grow in this freedom, it has become my life's calling to help others discover that same place of liberty.

That's where I hope *unstuck* comes in for you. Maybe this is your time for freedom. I sure hope so. It's worth it to be "all in" to what God has for you in the pages ahead. No worries though. God knows what He is up to in your life, and it's all good.

## — MY PRAYER FOR YOU —

*Father, I thank You that freedom in Your Son, Jesus, is real and meant for every one of Your children, young or old, man or woman. You love each of us far beyond what we can know or understand and I pray You would powerfully reveal Your love through these studies. Please spread Your protection over those going through this book and turn on the lights in their minds and hearts. Bring joy where there has been discouragement and victory where there has been defeat. And where they are trapped or stalled out in faith, send forth your Spirit of grace and truth and enable them to get unstuck... truly free in Christ. Amen.*

# what is freedom in Christ?
## EXPERIENCING YOUR NEW LIFE

## what is freedom?

Freedom is a really big deal here in America. Our Declaration of Independence says that we are endowed by our Creator with certain unalienable rights... including life, liberty and the pursuit of happiness. Our national anthem says we are "the land of the free and the home of the brave." Even New Hampshire's state motto shouts the message, "Live Free or Die!"

## what does it mean to be "free?"

**>> Take a few minutes and brainstorm in your group about what you think a good definition of "freedom" would be. Write your thoughts below.**

_____

_____

_____

_____

_____

_____

_____

**>> Take a minute and think about the following statement. Do you believe it is true or false? Why? Write your conclusion in the blank space below the statement. Then discuss your answer with your group.**

## FREEDOM IS BEING ABLE TO DO WHATEVER YOU WANT WHENEVER YOU WANT.

_____

_____

_____

_____

The statement above (freedom is being able to do whatever you want whenever you want) sounds pretty good, doesn't it? I suspect a lot of people would say this is what freedom is and ought to be. However, when you think about it, if that statement were actually believed and followed, "freedom" could get really messy, really fast. Imagine just one person trying to live out that philosophy of life suddenly meeting up with one other person trying to live out their own version of that philosophy of life. That's a conflict just waiting to happen. Multiply that many times over and it's called war!

## FREEDOM SOMEHOW HAS TO BE SOMETHING DIFFERENT THAN SIMPLY DOING YOUR OWN THING.

**» Let's shift our attention to the main question of our first study, "What is freedom in Christ?" Before we look at what God has to say about this subject, take a crack at coming up with your own definition of what "freedom in Christ" is. Don't worry at this point whether your definition is right or wrong; we're just getting started. So give it your best shot and share what you came up with those in your group.**

**I think freedom in Christ is...**

_____

_____

_____

_____

_____

As we get rolling here, I think it would first be helpful to know if "freedom" and "Christ" actually are connected in the Bible, because many people who call themselves Christians seem to be anything but free. Maybe you've met some people like that. They say they are followers of Christ but act like they gargled with vinegar before coming to church on Sunday mornings!

Okay, let's see what God has to say about the subject:

*It was for freedom that Christ set us free; therefore keep standing firm and do not be subject again to a yoke of slavery.*
GALATIANS 5:1

*Therefore there is now no condemnation for those who are in Christ Jesus. For the law of the Spirit of life in Christ Jesus has set you free from the law of sin and of death.*
ROMANS 8:1,2

*So Jesus was saying to those Jews who had believed Him, "If you continue in My word, then you are truly disciples of Mine; and you will know the truth, and the truth will make you free." They answered Him, "We are Abraham's descendants and have never been enslaved to anyone; how is it that You say, 'You will become free.' Jesus answered them, 'Truly, truly, I say to you, everyone who commits sin is the slave of sin...So if the Son makes you free, you will be free indeed.'"*
JOHN 8:31-36

**» Discuss the following questions based on the three quotes from the Bible above. Write the conclusions from your group in the space provided:**

**Does the Bible indicate that Jesus has anything to do with our freedom? If so, in what way?**

_____
_____
_____
_____

**What is it that we need to be set free from?**

_____
_____

_____

_____

_____

**Based on John 8:31-36, is "knowing the Bible" enough for us to be free, or is more needed? Explain your answer.**

_____

_____

_____

_____

I hope you were able to come up with some answers. Here's my take on those questions:

The Bible couldn't be clearer. Jesus has a lot to do with freedom. In fact, He came to set us free from the controlling power of sin. How does He do that? We experience freedom through knowing the truth, according to John 8:32. Notice I didn't say, through "knowing the Bible."

*Scared you, didn't I?*

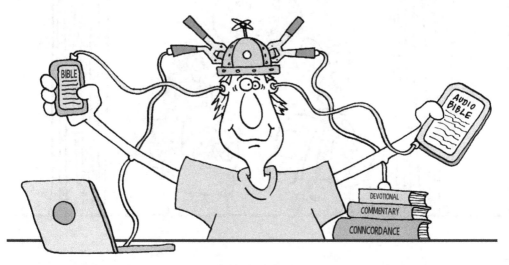

Bible Knowledge

Don't worry. I fully believe that studying the Word of God is essential to being a true follower of Jesus. No question about it. But there is more to "the truth" than the Bible alone. Jesus Himself is the truth (see John 14:6) and if He sets you free, you will really be free (John 8:36). Somebody could have most if not all of the Bible memorized and be an atheist, you know. The devil himself knows the Bible better than you do and he's certainly not free! So, knowing the truth of God's Word plus knowing the Truth Himself (Jesus) are needed for freedom from sin.

You've likely heard this statement before: The truth will set you free. In fact, many universities have carved or mounted that statement on their halls of higher education. But Jesus wasn't talking about academics when He made that statement. When you take all of what Jesus said in John 8:31-36, it is clear He was talking about His words working in close relationship to His Person bringing His freedom from sin's control in our lives.

**»  This is a very important point, so go ahead and discuss the following questions in your group:**

**What do you think could happen if someone truly knew Jesus as Savior and wanted the Spirit of Christ to speak to his/her heart, but didn't spend much time in God's Word?**

_____

_____

_____

_____

_____

**What do you think could happen if someone spent lots of time studying the Bible, but did not have a true and close relationship with the person of Christ Himself?**

_____

_____

_____

_____

_____

The issues raised by those two questions are very important, because there are many people who tend toward one of those two extremes.

In the first case, the person may be very zealous for Christ and the working of the Holy Spirit in a mystical sort of way, but could be dangerously open to deception because the truth of God's Word is not richly dwelling in his or her mind and heart. It is possible to elevate one's own thoughts, other religious books or even false visions and revelations from the powers of darkness to an equal authority with the Bible if the Word of God is not known and respected as a plumb line of truth.

In the second case, the person could become cold, hard, proud and judgmental. He or she might be filled with a lot of Bible knowledge but have a heart empty of the compassionate touch of the gentle, humble Jesus. College, university and even seminary degrees can be very helpful, but apart from the presence of Christ, knowledge puffs up and makes people arrogant, but Christ's love builds us up and keeps us humble (see 1 Corinthians 8:1).

In neither of these cases is the person truly free.

**Remember...**

We're still on a quest to try and determine a good, biblical definition of "freedom in Christ." Before we come to that point and bring this first study to a close, we need to discuss one more issue...

Take a look at the following statement:

## THE CHRISTIAN LIFE IS WELL-SUMMED UP AS "TRYING HARD TO OBEY GOD'S COMMANDS."

>> In the space below, write your opinion of the statement, "The Christian life is well-summed up as trying hard to obey God's commands." Do you agree or disagree with it? Why? Discuss what you think with those in your group.

_____

_____

_____

_____

Did you agree with that statement? If you did, you are not alone. In preparation for the writing of the book, *Grace That Breaks the Chains*, the authors contracted with the (George) Barna Research Group who conducted a scientific survey of Christian believers. A full 82% of those surveyed agreed with that statement, with 57% strongly agreeing.

Maybe you noticed that there are some big problems with that definition of the Christian life. Why? Because some very significant pieces are missing in it, like: Jesus, Holy Spirit, faith (trust), grace, relationship, love... you know, minor issues like that!

Actually, that statement about the Christian life from the Barna survey does not define the Christian life at all. It defines legalism. Legalism is a religious system that teaches one must perform really hard and really well in order for God to truly love and accept you. In legalism one must jump through numerous "religious or spiritual hoops" in order to gain or maintain God's favor. It involves trying hard to make the Christian life work, rather than trusting Him to make it work in and through you. Sadly, many who seek to follow Christ live in this way.

Let's go back to that false definition of Christianity that's a lie: The Christian life is well-summed up as "Trying hard to obey God's commands."

**>> Discuss the following questions in your group:**

**What kind of person would somebody be if they truly believed that statement (The Christian life is well-summed up as "Trying hard to obey God's commands")? What would their Christian life be like? Would such a person truly be free, in your opinion?**

_____

_____

_____

_____

**In all honesty, do you ever find yourself believing and living as if that statement were true? If so, why do you think that you have come to believe and live that way?**

_____

_____

_____

_____

You probably have rightly concluded that a person who believes and lives this way is not likely a joyful, uninhibited worshiper, seeker and follower of God. He or she would tend to be filled with anxiety, feeling guilty or ashamed, likely possessing a drivenness to perform for God and people that would burden and eventually crush their spirits. Either that or they would be proud, self-righteous and a pain in the neck to be around, thinking they were doing exactly what God expected, viewing themselves as some sort of Bible superhero.

## Captain Knowledge

Are you beginning to see the power of a lie? Can you see how we need to know the truth to set us free? This is a crucial statement:

### KNOWING THE TRUTH SETS US FREE; BELIEVING LIES KEEPS US IN BONDAGE!

**»** **Discuss in your group an example from your life when you believed something that wasn't true and believing that lie made you angry, anxious or depressed or got you in some kind of trouble.**

What would happen if the same person who believed that lie of legalism came to believe instead that they were already unconditionally loved, totally accepted, completely forgiven and fully secure in Jesus? Rather than trying hard to obey God in their own strength, they would find themselves excited about keeping His commands through the power of the Holy Spirit living inside them! This person would be well on the way to experiencing freedom in Christ.

Okay... so finally... let's have a go at coming up with a definition of "freedom in Christ."

First, the "elevator conversation" version:

**Freedom in Christ is becoming mentally, emotionally
and spiritually "unstuck" to live life as God intended.**

You might find the simplicity of that version very helpful. If so, keep it on the back burner of your brain. However, for the purposes of gaining more in-depth understanding, here's the more complete definition we'll use in these studies:

---

**Freedom in Christ is overcoming sin's power and the devil's lies through repentance and faith in the truth, joyfully living in the fullness of the Holy Spirit as a secure, loved, accepted and significant child of the God of grace.**

---

I know that's a mouthful, but it is important to be thorough enough to cover the main bases. We'll unpack this definition and focus on different parts of it in the studies to come. For now...

**≫ Take a few minutes in your group and discuss that second definition. Do you agree with it? If not, what would you change? What parts of it sound really good to you? Which parts would you say you are experiencing now? Which parts do you struggle to consistently live out?**

_____

_____

_____

_____

_____

Now, we will never experience freedom in Christ 100% of the time this side of heaven. But to see freedom be increasingly true in your life, doesn't that sound good? Isn't that what you truly want out of life?

**Wouldn't it be great to be able to get unstuck from:**

- negative, critical, doom and gloom moods
- secretive behaviors and addictions that wrap you in coils of guilt, shame and fear
- racing, obsessive thoughts that rob you of rest
- angry outbursts that blast those around you, damaging those you love
- dark, smoldering, revengeful thoughts that are turning your heart hard or bitter
- worries and anxieties that steal your joy
- fears that paralyze you and keep you from exploring and enjoying a life of faith
- apathetic, lazy, unmotivated attitudes that paint the Christian life as boring and everything else as exciting
- an argumentative, contentious spirit that is stressing out your friends and family and sabotaging relationships that are important to you
- busyness, ambition and greed that are rewarding you with a good living... while eating you alive on the inside with empty loneliness
- fantasies and imaginations that are pulling you into a world of unreality and which are making the real world look dull

- Other plaguing problems in your life you would like to be rid of: _____

_____

_____

≫ Think about the things that have a hold on you. If any of them are listed above, put a mark next to those items. Make your own list below ours if the Lord brings something else to your mind. Then try and be brave and discuss at least one of those things you checked with members of your group. Pray for one another about these things and keep what is shared in the group confidential within the group.

You need to know that the things that have a hold on you don't have to control you anymore. Christ came to set captives free to become growing, fruitful disciples. Maybe you are one of those captives that He wants to release from slavery. He's got His eye on you, not to condemn you (see Romans 8:1), but to bring you into freedom in Christ. He only asks for your cooperation and willingness to let Him do His work. Will you let Him?

That is actually a very crucial question and your answer will largely determine how much or how little an impact these studies will have on your life.

I'll conclude this week's lesson with a Scripture and a prayer:

*Therefore, since we have so great a cloud of witnesses surrounding us, let us also lay aside every encumbrance and the sin which so easily entangles us, and let us run with endurance the race that is set before us, fixing our eyes on Jesus, the author and perfecter of faith...*
HEBREWS 12:1-2A

## PRAY

*Dear heavenly Father, it is humbling enough to admit I need help, but it really hurts my ego to admit that I'm helpless to experience freedom without You. Sin is too strong for me; it always has been. Maybe I'm just beginning to see that or be willing to see it. Freedom sounds really good. It sounds clean and pure and powerful and fresh. I know it's what I want deep down, but frankly I'm scared. I'm afraid that changing might be really hard and even painful. I need You to walk with me and enable me to overcome these areas that are weighing me down and tripping me up. But I guess that's what You are here for. I know that is the only way to live a life that truly glorifies You and that's what I want, too, even though there's still a part of me that thinks some sin looks pretty good. Whatever it takes, Lord, to bring me into the fullness of freedom in Christ, I'm ready... or at least I think I am. Be my strength and carry me on this journey. In Jesus' name I pray. Amen.*

# who are you?

## EXPERIENCING YOUR NEW IDENTITY IN CHRIST

In our first study, we explored what "freedom in Christ" actually is. After looking at a number of Bible verses and discussing their meanings, we came up with:

> Freedom in Christ is overcoming sin's power and the devil's lies through repentance and faith in the truth, joyfully living in the fullness of the Holy Spirit as a secure, loved, accepted and significant child of the God of grace.

As we said before, perfect 100% sinless freedom here on earth... that the Lord Jesus experienced... is not possible for us. Unfortunately, all of us will commit sins until the day we die. But a life of increasing freedom and maturity in Christ is not only possible, but it is God's will for you and me (see Galatians 5:1 and Romans 8:28,29).

In this second study we will fast forward and look at the last part of that definition of "freedom in Christ," because without a rock solid foundation of seeing ourselves as a "secure, loved, accepted and significant child of the God of grace" there simply cannot be true freedom. So let's jump in and get to know you... the real you... in Christ. First, an easy exercise to get started:

My online dating profile.

>> How would you describe yourself? Imagine that you were filling out an application for a job and that was the question they asked. How would you respond? Write your response below and share what you wrote with the others in your discipleship group. It will help them get to know you a little bit better anyway.

_____

_____

_____

_____

If you are a typical person, you likely wrote about things like your age, family background, education, accomplishments, personality, skills, talents, employment experience... that sort of thing. And, of course, that would be completely appropriate for a job application. Maybe you were bold enough to identify yourself as a Christian or at least mentioned that you were a church-goer, if that happens to be the case.

>> Here are a couple other questions to think about and discuss in your group. They hit a bit closer to home, I know, but I'd like you to give them a

shot anyway. It'll feel good to be honest. It feels even better to be honest in an environment of acceptance without criticism or judgment. I hope your group is that kind of safe place.

Are there any aspects of your appearance, background or personality that you would change if you could? If so, what would you change? Why would you like to change it?

_____

_____

_____

_____

No matter how you answered the previous questions, the one question you need to be able to accurately answer in order to get to know the real you is this one: **How would *God* describe you?** Take a stab at answering that question. Is it possible that God's description of you might be a bit different from your description of you? How you answer this question is really important. *Answer according to what you really believe and feel deep down.* In other words, be totally honest and write your answer according to how you truly perceive God's view of you to be, not necessarily what you think the "right" answer should be.

To give you a jump start, I've listed quite a few different statements that you can choose from. Check the ones that best describe how you picture God describing you right now. Write your own in the "Other" section if our statements don't quite capture how you feel.

**»** Once you are done, talk about what you wrote with the others in your group.

### How I believe... deep down... God really feels about me:

☐   You are a loser. You can't do anything right

☐   When are you going to get it? You might as well give up. You'll never change.

☐   When you are good, I bless you. When you are not, I turn My back.

- ☐ I love you as much as I love My Son, Jesus.

- ☐ I am powerfully at work in you to make you all I've created you to be.

- ☐ I'm sick to death of how easily you give in to sin.

- ☐ You are holy, a saint.

- ☐ I chose you to be My child and have gladly made you a part of My family.

- ☐ I'm too busy with more important things than to waste My time on you.

- ☐ You are on your own as far as I'm concerned.

- ☐ I am holding on to your hand; you are safe with Me.

- ☐ I have specifically hand-picked gifts and abilities for you to have and use.

- ☐ I get excited when you succeed.

- ☐ One more time of messing up, and it's over. I've had it up to here with you!

- ☐ You are My delight, the apple of My eye!

- ☐ Others that come to your mind that you want to add: _____

    _____

    _____

One of the hardest things for us to realize is that "how we feel" does not always line up with the truth. Our feelings can seem so true, but just because something *feels* true doesn't mean it *is* true. I'm not saying what you feel isn't *real*. You may *really feel* discouraged, unloved, abandoned, rejected, alone, powerless, etc. Those feelings are very real. But not everything that is real to us necessarily corresponds to reality. Does that make sense?

Maybe an example will help make this clear. In my life there have been days when I've felt very alone, as if God was nowhere to be found. The feeling was very real, I was not imagining it. But was it true? Was that feeling an accurate reflection of reality? For some reason had God gone off on vacation or, worse yet, turned His back on me? What was I going to use to gauge whether what I was feeling was true or not? Knowing that God's Word is truth (John 17:17), I checked out Hebrews 13:5 where God says, "I will never leave you. I will never forsake you."

So, the feelings were very *real*, but they were also very *wrong*. God could not have been closer. I just couldn't *feel* Him.

The same can be (and very often is) the case when it comes to how we think God views us. You might have checked all the negative statements up above and feel in the deepest part of your gut that those statements are exactly how God feels about you. It's very possible that negative "labels" slapped onto your soul – like "stupid", "loser", "ugly", "unlovable", "dirty", "evil", "worthless" and so on, have functioned as "curses" on your life. As curses they have effectively stifled any growth of confidence in God or belief that He could use you. Even though you read in the Bible that God loves you, deep down you may believe that He dislikes you intensely or, at best, tolerates you.

How about we let God speak for Himself? Let Him express His view of you in His own words. Look over the following Scriptures and recognize that each one of them is completely true of you... right now... if you are a true believer in Christ.

>> **Underline everything the following verses say about God's people. Then tell your group which truth(s) mean the most to you and why.**

*But you are a chosen race, a royal priesthood, a holy nation, a people for God's own possession, so that you may proclaim the excellencies of Him who has called you out of darkness into His marvelous light; for you once were not a people, but now you are the people of God; you had not received mercy, but now you have received mercy.*
1 PETER 2:9,10

*The LORD your God is in your midst, a victorious warrior. He will exult over you with joy, He will be quiet in His love, He will rejoice over you with shouts of joy.*
ZEPHANIAH 3:17

*[Jesus talking to the Father about us] The glory which You have given Me I have given to them, that they may be one, just as We are one; I in them and You in Me that they may be perfected in unity, so that the world may know that You sent Me, and loved them, even as You have loved Me.*

JOHN 17:22,23

*See how great a love the Father has bestowed on us, that we would be called children of God; and such we are. For this reason the world does not know us, because it did not know Him. Beloved, now we are children of God, and it has not appeared as yet what we will be. We know that when He appears, we will be like Him, because we will see Him just as He is.*
1 JOHN 3:1,2

*Grace to you and peace, from Him who is and who was and who is to come, and from the seven Spirits who are before His throne, and from Jesus Christ, the faithful witness, the firstborn of the dead, and the ruler of the kings of the earth. To Him who loves us and released us from our sins by His blood— and He has made us to be a kingdom, priests to His God and Father.–*
REVELATION 1:4-6A

And those Bible verses are just the beginning! There are many more passages of Scripture that proclaim that God is really on our side, rooting for us to succeed, loving us deeply, as a good Father loves His kids. It is amazing to realize that every one of those things you underlined in the Scriptures above is true... about you... right now, if you are a follower of Jesus!

## WHY NOT ASK GOD TO HELP YOU BELIEVE THEM?

The next project could be very meaningful to you. Write a short note to thank God for how He really sees you—with eyes of purest, deepest love. If you are used to sending text messages, you can imagine you are texting God. That's totally cool. Be specific with the things you are thanking Him for, using some truths from those Scriptures above. You might even need to tell God you are sorry for any lies that you have believed about yourself and Him.

**>> When you are in your group, go ahead and read your note of thanks to God out loud as a prayer. I bet your honesty will encourage someone else.**

| Note (text) of thanks to God: |
| --- |

_____

_____

_____

_____

_____

_____

_____

**>> What was that project like for you? Was it encouraging or did you feel like you were just going through the motions? Did you find yourself struggling with any old labels or "memory tapes" that broadcast loudly that you are a failure, worthless, unlovable, etc.? Sometimes those can drown out the truth of God's Word. In your group, discuss your answers to these questions, then ask the Lord to begin shining light on why it is hard for you at times to believe what God's Word says is true of you.**

Maybe I can help you with that question. To unlock the mystery of why we struggle to believe what is true of us in Christ, we need to talk about **rejection**.

All of us get criticized at times. We mess up and others let us know they are not happy with what we've done. We may be laughed at, scolded, rebuked, corrected, and so on. That is a part of life, and though it may be embarrassing or even humiliating for a while, we usually get over it. We get up and try harder or we discover something else we are good at, in order to feel better about ourselves again. Sometimes we don't get over it. We feel stupid, incompetent, unwanted, unimportant, unloved. We feel rejected and we can't seem to shake that feeling.

## REJECTION RUNS DEEP. REJECTION DOES NOT INVOLVE WHAT WE DO BUT WHO WE ARE.

There are two kinds of rejection that we will very briefly look at. The first type is *open rejection*, the kind that is "in your face" obvious. Open rejection is the negation of you as a person. People turn their backs on you, ignore you, exclude you, or ostracize you because they have devalued you to the point where, in their eyes, you are worth little or worthless.

Think of a time when you were openly rejected. What happened? Can you remember what was going on in your mind and your feelings at the time? What did you do in order to try and handle the rejection? Did it work?

**» Write down a summary of that incident in the space provided below, and try and talk about this incident in your group. Maybe you've never talked about this with anybody, so it might be hard to bring it up. But usually we feel a lot better once we get things like this off our chest.**

_____

_____

_____

_____

_____

_____

*The following illustration may help you understand how experiencing rejection can affect your ability to believe God's truth about you.*

Imagine you take the purest bottled water and pour it into a coffee maker that has stale coffee grounds in the filter. What is going to come out is some foul-colored, foul-tasting stuff... Seattle's worst coffee.

God's Word is the pure water. The stale coffee grounds are your memories of rejection. In the process of trying to bring the pure water of God's truth by faith into your heart, the "water" drips through your rejection-memories and your stale belief system about yourself. And so a truth like "you are deeply loved by God" becomes in your mind "Yeah right. Nobody has ever given a rip about me and neither does God." Or you may read in the Bible that God will be with you always, but your mind tells you, "For as long as I can remember, I've been on my own. It's no different now."

I think you get the picture. The "stale coffee grounds" are distorting God's truth in your thinking. God's Word is still true but you have a very hard time believing it because that truth is being colored and tainted by the wounds of rejection in your heart. It is not uncommon for a person who has suffered much rejection to think, "Sure, it's true for everybody else, but not for me" when the Bible presents any kind of positive, encouraging words.

The problem is not the "pure water." The problem is the stale coffee grounds.

**That's the first type of rejection. But there is another way rejection occurs apart from "open rejection."**

Maybe as you think back in your life, you have been largely successful, pretty well-liked and rarely (if ever) openly rejected. You may not be able to relate to the "open rejection" we just talked about. But you still may have experienced a form of rejection.

There is a second type of rejection that actually masquerades as acceptance. It is called *"performance-based acceptance"* which means that people express love to you only when you are good or when you succeed or win or reach some level of achievement (athletically, artistically, academically, financially, vocationally, etc.).

People who have lived life under "performance-based acceptance" can outwardly appear quite confident, even cocky, but inside they may be deeply insecure. Why? Because love has always come with strings attached, with a price tag on it.

Does God only dole out His love to those who can jump through certain religious hoops? Does God smile at you when you're a "good boy or girl" but turn away in disgust when you're not? Does God care only for those who get A-pluses on their spiritual report card? Absolutely not!

God's love for those who, through Christ, are His children is unconditional. So whether you have been rejected openly by those who have excluded you or been rejected subtly through "performance-based acceptance", here's the truth:

*In Christ, God loves and accepts you just as you are, right now. He loves you when you're good. He loves you when you're not. He loves you before you sin. He loves you after you sin. He loves you even while you are sinning. Though He hates the sin itself, He will never reject you. "There is therefore now no condemnation for those who are in Christ Jesus" (Romans 8:1)! "No" means no. "Now" means now. In Christ, you are a safe, secure, completely forgiven and deeply loved child of the God of grace. And nothing can ever change that. Nothing.*

How can that be? It's simple really. God loves us because God is love (1 John 4:16). It is His nature to love. That's just how He is and who He is. His love for us, then, is based on His unchanging character, not based on our ever-changing behavior. I don't know about you, but for me that is very good news. Nothing we do or don't do affects His desire or ability to love us. He loves us... period.

>> Take a few minutes and talk about those last two paragraphs in your group. Do you believe what is written there? Does it seem too good to be true? Is there a counter-thought saying to you, "Yeah, but..."?

Too often the good fruit in our lives is trampled on and consumed by what I call "the little gray yeahbut's" in our minds. Rather than listening to those varmints, we ought to take out our spiritual shotguns and blast the little suckers!

"Open Season on Yeahbuts"

≫ After your discussion, read out loud and think about the verses from the Bible that are on the following page. They are all about God's love for us and they are absolutely true, even when people reject us. No matter how terrible we might feel about ourselves due to rejection by people, God's love for us never fails. God's love for us never changes. God's love for us never ends.

*What, then, shall we say in response to these things? If God is for us, who can be against us? He who did not spare his own Son, but gave him up for us all—how will he not also, along with him, graciously give us all things? Who will bring any charge against those whom God has chosen? It is God who justifies. Who then is the one who condemns? No one. Christ Jesus who died—more than that, who was raised to life—is at the right hand of God and is also interceding for us. Who shall separate us from the love of Christ? Shall trouble or hardship or persecution or famine or nakedness or danger or sword? As it is written: "For your sake we face death all day long; we are considered as sheep to be slaughtered." No, in all these things we are more than conquerors through him who loved us. For I am convinced that neither death nor life, neither angels nor demons, neither the present nor the future, nor any powers, neither height nor depth, nor anything else in all creation, will be able to separate us from the love of God that is in Christ Jesus our Lord.*

ROMANS 8:31-39 NIV

## PRAY

*Father, Your Word is amazing. It's incredibly pure and refreshing like the coldest water on the hottest, driest day of my soul. Some of it I believe; other parts are not so easy to swallow. I guess I've still got some stale coffee grounds in my heart that I need You to remove. I want to come to the point of being able to fully receive the truth that I am a completely accepted, deeply loved, totally secure child of the God of grace. I reject the lie that You relate to me according to "performance-based acceptance." Your love does not fluctuate like the Dow Jones Average based on how well my "spiritual stock" is performing that day. Your love and acceptance of me are according to "Jesus-based performance." Because He never did anything wrong and I am in Him, You see me with the same eyes of love and acceptance as You see Your Son. Regardless of what my feelings may be shouting at me right now, I choose to believe Your truth. Thanks for helping me get to know me a little better today. I choose to believe that what You say about me is true. Amen.*

# where are you?

## EXPERIENCING YOUR NEW POSITION IN CHRIST

At the risk of being "redundantly repetitive", let's review the definition of "freedom in Christ" that we are unpacking, bit by bit, in each study:

> Freedom in Christ is overcoming sin's power and the devil's lies through repentance and faith in the truth, joyfully living in the fullness of the Holy Spirit as a secure, loved, accepted and significant child of the God of grace.

As I have said before, we will not experience that freedom every moment of every day. But, through God's grace, we can find "freedom in Christ" increasingly true of our lives. And when we blow it and sin (and if you don't think that is still a problem, just ask your best friend!) we can always come back to God in confession, knowing that the blood of Jesus cleanses us from all sin (1 John 1:7-9).

In our last study we looked at our new identity in Christ. I hope you were able to catch a fresh glimpse of the truth that in Christ you are *a secure, loved, accepted and significant child of the God of grace*. However, if the truths from last week are still hard for you to believe, hang in there. Keep your heart open to God and trust that He is working in you. He is (see Philippians 2:13).

In this third study, we are going to look at our new **position** in Christ, the place of *overcoming sin's power... through repentance.* Ask God to teach you what He knows you need to learn from this study:

*Dear heavenly Father, I know Jesus won a total victory over temptation and sin. As a follower of Jesus, teach me how to increasingly experience that same freedom from sin's power and control that Christ had. Though I know I will never achieve perfection in this life, I want to live my life overcoming the power of sin more each day. Through Jesus I pray with faith. Amen.*

Our position in Christ is what enables us, as our definition above states, to live life with the increasing ability to overcome sin's power. I'll explain more about what being "in Christ" means in a few minutes.

Living life with the increasing ability to overcome sin's power may sound like a real stretch to you. You may be saying to yourself, "I'd settle for just a few minutes without sin calling the shots in my life." A lot of people, if they were honest with themselves, would say the same thing. Others might struggle with putting their finger on any areas of sin in their lives. (What those folks need is an outspoken three-year-old to hang out with them for a day!)

35

Either way, I think this next exercise will be eye opening for you.

To get started, take a look at the following list. Which areas are struggles for you? Be honest. Maybe you are not used to taking a head-on look at the areas of selfishness and sin in your life, but that's okay. Now is a great time to start, so go ahead and check off the ones that are problems in your life.

**>> If you are comfortable doing so, tell those in your group one or two areas where you struggle. Take the time to pray for each other. What is talked about in your group stays in your group. Respecting confidentiality is crucial to building trust in an environment of openness and honesty—something that is essential for our spiritual health.**

## Stuff I struggle with:

- [ ] losing my temper
- [ ] keeping quiet and not honestly expressing my opinions for fear of displeasing people
- [ ] fretting and worrying about stuff too much
- [ ] struggling with substance abuse or addictions
- [ ] being fascinated and captivated by cruel, gruesomely violent or dark horror stories or occult practices
- [ ] harboring resentment toward people who have hurt me
- [ ] talking about people behind their backs
- [ ] quietly or overtly refusing to do what someone in authority tells me to do
- [ ] getting so wrapped up in a job, hobbies, TV, etc. so that God, family or rest is neglected
- [ ] loving sports or personal fitness more than God
- [ ] finding that pornography or other sexual sins have a stronger grip on me than I'd like to admit

☐   loving money and the things it can buy

☐   alienating people around me because of my harsh, critical words

☐   withdrawing from relationships and retreating into a world of computer or video games, TV, music, books, internet

☐   doing stuff (even in church) to be noticed, respected, complimented, etc.

☐   not really caring a whole lot about reading my Bible, praying, going to church, telling others about Jesus, etc.

☐   being reluctant or unwilling to even try to reconcile with someone I am at odds with

Okay, let's stop there. There are not enough pages in this book to describe all the possible ways sin might be entrapping and enslaving you. The important thing to realize is that you can change because God wants you to change. God wants *you* to change. That's one of the reasons why Christ came... to set captives free to become growing, fruitful disciples.

Too often we keep our struggles pent up inside. Our fear and pride keep us from telling anyone else. So we end up stuck in secret sin which leads to secret defeat, which leads to secret shame and even greater isolation, which leads to more secret sin, defeat and shame. We find ourselves spiraling downward, getting trapped deeper and deeper—not knowing how to get out.

**We're stuck.**

**We need to get** unstuck.

Sometimes all it takes to begin to turn things around is to finally tell someone. Really. I hope you are able to do that in your group. We all need to find at least one wise, trustworthy person with whom we can be honest and real. We all need at least one good friend.

The following Bible verses are great words of hope...that predict what the Messiah, the Lord Jesus Christ would come to do... written hundreds of years before He was born in Bethlehem:

> *The Spirit of the Lord God is upon me, because the Lord has anointed me to bring good news to the afflicted; He has sent me to bind up the brokenhearted, to proclaim liberty to captives and freedom to prisoners; to proclaim the favorable year of the Lord and the day of vengeance of our God; to comfort all who mourn, to grant those who mourn in Zion, giving them a garland instead of ashes, the oil of gladness instead of mourning, the mantle of praise instead of a spirit of fainting. So they will be called oaks of righteousness, the planting of the Lord, that He may be glorified.*
> ISAIAH 61:1-3

God is looking for people who are mourning over their sin, not people who are justifying it and making excuses for it or who are denying it. Those who are mourning, He will comfort. Those who are trapped in sin, He will rescue. The result? We become strong "oaks of righteousness"—right thinking, right living. And God gets the honor and credit He deserves!

**≫ How does a person get out of slavery to sin? How do you start to experience the "liberty to captives" and "freedom to prisoners" which Isaiah predicted Jesus would give? Below are some of the possible ways of escaping sin's clutches. Check the ones you've tried. Comment after each one how well that activity worked; then talk about what you wrote below with those in your group.**

## Ways I've tried to escape sin's clutches

☐ read the Bible more

_____

_____

☐ pray more

_____

_____

☐ go to church more

_____

_____

☐ seek accountability
_____
_____

☐ confess sins publicly
_____
_____

☐ fast
_____
_____

☐ go to counseling
_____
_____

☐ witness more
_____
_____

☐ serve harder in the church
_____
_____

☐ plead to God with tears
_____
_____

☐ read books / check out websites about sin and
how to defeat it
_____
_____

☐ attend a class or conference on that issue
_____
_____

☐ go to a support group
_____
_____

Now, there's nothing wrong with those things listed above, when done for the right reasons. And hopefully you have found some level of encouragement or at least relief through one or more of these practices. But to think that by simply doing something different or even something religious you can be free from being held captive by sin... well forget it! It doesn't work that way.

> *Trying to find freedom from sin by changing how you <u>behave</u> will NOT work (at least not for long) until you first change what you <u>believe</u>. A change in how you believe or think is called **repentance**. To "repent" means literally to "change your mind." That change of thinking, if genuinely coming from the heart, will result in a genuine change of behavior (see Matthew 3:8).*

And so we come to the subject of our **position** in Christ. Your identity in Christ (our last study) tells you "who you are." Your position in Christ tells you "where you are."

Before you tune me out and conclude I'm some kind of nutcase for trying to tell you where you are, when you know very well where you are and you know I don't know where you are, hear me out. I'm not talking about the location of your body. I'm talking about your spiritual position. And the Bible tells us that every true follower of Jesus is *in Christ*.

### So what does it mean to be "in Christ"?

Maybe this illustration will help.

As human beings, we are basically stuck on planet earth, with our feet planted firmly on the ground, because of gravity. Gravity exerts a constant influence on us, whether we are conscious of it or not. Though you and I can jump off the ground, our experience of being airborne is brief. We cannot fly. That is, unless we are *in an airplane*. As long as we are in that airplane, we can overcome gravity's "glue" that sticks our feet to the earth's surface. It's the same thing in our relationship with Christ. Without Him, this world and all it offers keep us locked in sin. But *in Christ* we can soar above sin's "gravitational pull." We can overcome sin's power.

Now, if you have been a Christian for any length of time, you have probably heard that Christ is *in you*. But have you ever heard that you are *in Christ*? Jesus said that both truths would be important for us to know:

*In that day you will know that I am in My Father, and you in Me, and I in you.*
JOHN 14:20

In order to understand what it means to be in Christ, think of being "in union" with Him or united to Him, connected to Him in a very powerful way spiritually. You are "in the plane", so to speak.

*But the one who joins himself to the Lord is one spirit with Him.*
1 CORINTHIANS 6:17

There is a dynamic, though invisible, connection between us and our Lord that has powerful implications in our battle against sin. To understand this truth is to discover the foundation of our freedom from sin's power and control. The Bible also says:

*I have been crucified with Christ; and it is no longer I who live, but Christ lives in me; and the life which I now live in the flesh I live by faith in the Son of God who loved me and gave Himself up for me.*
GALATIANS 2:20

*For if we have become united with Him in the likeness of His death, certainly we shall also be in the likeness of His resurrection, knowing this, that our old self was crucified with Him, in order that our body of sin might be done away with, so that we would no longer be slaves to sin; for he who has died is freed from sin.*
ROMANS 6:5-7

**>> Take a few minutes in your group and discuss what you think these two passages from the Bible mean. It might help to put them in your own words. How do they relate to your struggles against sin? How do these truths give us hope for victory over sin... today?**

As remarkable and even unbelievable as the previous Scriptures may sound, they are absolutely true... today... for all who are "in Christ." Let's sum up what they are saying:

- When Christ died on the cross, our old self that loved sin died... it really died.

- We are different people now; we are in Christ and He is in us.

- We have not only been united to Christ in His death, but also in His resurrection power and life.

- We are now dead to sin; sin has lost its control. Its stranglehold over our lives is gone!

## THIS IS YOUR SPIRITUAL EMANCIPATION PROCLAMATION!

So what is our responsibility? How does this work exactly? Let's read on in Romans 6:

*Even so consider yourselves to be dead to sin, but alive to God in Christ Jesus. Therefore do not let sin reign in your mortal body so that you obey its lusts, and do not go on presenting the members of your body to sin as instruments of unrighteousness; but present yourselves to God as those alive from the dead, and your members as instruments of righteousness to God. For sin shall not be master over you, for you are not under law but under grace.*

ROMANS 6:11-14

Dead to sin? What in the world does that mean? Basically, in Christ sin no longer has the power to force you to do its bidding. You are no longer its slave. Sure, sin is still around (just like gravity still exists on the airplane... you walk down the aisle to the restroom; you don't float!), but you are free from its cruel dictatorship. As long as you remain *in the airplane*, you overcome gravity's effect. You fly. Should you ever decide to take a stroll on the wing of the plane at 30,000 feet, you would soon be reminded of how powerful gravity is!

Chances are you have thought temptation and sin were too strong for you. Without Christ, that's totally true. But in Christ, it is just the opposite. Jesus defeated sin and in Him you have too. Your job is to count it true for you, because it is! Reject the lie that this is true for other "better" Christians, but not true for you. Remember, GOD said it. Believe it! Because of that reality, you can now make the choice to use your body for God's purposes rather than sin's purposes.

That's where the rubber meets the road.

Think of your body as a car, purchased by someone else and lent to you for your use. The owner wants you to use the car for good, but it's your choice. You can use the car to buy and sell street drugs or you can use it to take street people to church on Sunday. In the same way, "your body is a temple of the Holy Spirit who is in you, whom you have from God, and... you are not your own. For you have been bought with a price: therefore glorify God in your body" (1 Corinthians 6:19,20). You are free now to choose to use your body for "good" or for "no good."

©Mike Taylor, 2015

I think you get the picture.

This is extremely important because *every time* you sin, you use some part(s) of your body—even if it's just your brain. Every time you do something good, your body is involved as well.

>> **We want to help begin to make these truths practical for you. The following exercise has two parts to it. Fill them both out by writing your own prayers of confession and surrender and then discuss with your group which parts of this exercise were most helpful.**

**On the next page, you will see parts of your physical body listed. If the Lord shows you that you have been using a particular part of your body for sin's purposes, confess (admit) your sin. (For example, telling lies would be using your mouth for sin's purposes.) That is the first part. Next, yield (surrender) each part of your body back to God for His purposes. (For example, yielding your mouth to God to speak the truth in love). That is the second part. And that's what Romans 6:11-14 says to do.**

This could be a very liberating exercise for you, so take your time. First, pray the following prayer to invite God to direct you in this process...

*Dear Father in heaven, I know that You want me to use my body for what is good, but I also know that many times I have used my body for doing wrong instead. Please open my eyes to the ways I have used my body wrongly, so that I can confess those sins to You and surrender my body back to You for Your good use. Thank You that in Christ I am already forgiven but I need You to cleanse me of my sin. You bought me out of sin's slavery. I choose to use this body that You lent to me in a way that honors You. Amen.*

*We have included an example on the following page to get you started.*

---

## Confession of sin & surrender of the parts of my body to God

### BRAIN

*evil, cruel, selfish or lustful thoughts; fantasies; negative, controlling, critical or bitter attitudes; prejudices; lies believed; fears or anxieties that control; envy and jealousy*

---

**EX. CONFESSION:**

Father, I admit I have used my mind to come up with all kinds of nasty things that I could do to get back at (name the person) for saying those hurtful things to me. I know You are not happy with those revengeful thoughts and this destructive thinking. Thanks for forgiving me.

**SURRENDER:**

Lord, I now present my brain and mind to You so that I will think only on things that are true, honorable, right, pure, lovely and of good reputation about him/her. And I choose to forgive (name of person) for the pain he/she caused me. I choose to use my mind for Your glory, Lord!

Now it's your turn to write a prayer of **Confession** and **Surrender** of your brain (mind) to God...

**CONFESSION:**

**SURRENDER:**

>> Continue working through the exercise on the following pages, allowing God to reveal to you any parts of your body that have been used for sin's purposes. In your group, talk about some of the areas of struggles with sin you have had and pray for one another that Christ's victory over sin would become your victory over sin!

| MOUTH |
| :---: |

critical, judgmental words; gossip; slander; lies; verbal abuse; foul or lewd language or jokes; quarreling, overeating; eating disorders of any kind, etc.

**CONFESSION:**

SURRENDER:

## HANDS

*fighting; theft; physical abuse; unethical, violent or other illegal or criminal actions; greed and selfishness; vandalism; immoral use of computers, video games, etc.; sexual immorality (which involved the sexual organs as well); inappropriate or immoral touching*

CONFESSION:

SURRENDER:

## EYES

*pornography and other lewd materials; lusting over clothes, food, cars, homes, etc.; wasting time and energy on excessive TV and other things "pleasing to the eye"; lusting after others sexually, etc.*

**CONFESSION:**

**SURRENDER:**

## FEET

*places you go that are drawing or dragging you away from Christ*

**CONFESSION:**

SURRENDER:

---

### EARS

*music or other media, conversations entered into, websites visited etc. that are not "true, honorable, right, pure, lovely, of good reputation, excellent or worthy of praise" (see Phil. 4:8)*

---

CONFESSION:

SURRENDER:

Obviously, there are other parts of your body that get involved with sin—most notably sexual organs. If you have been involved with using your sexual organs in an immoral way, including having an abortion, confess those sins and surrender the sexual use of your body to God.

God through Christ, has taken away sin's power and control over us. The choice is truly yours now, because you are really free from sin's deadly dictatorship and you have been rescued into God's loving leadership. You can give your body to sin and be a slave. Or you can give your body to God and be free. If you still believe that your situation is hopeless or that you cannot give up a certain sin you are believing a lie, because no believer in Christ is a slave to sin.

Remember Romans 6:14, **"For sin shall not be master over you, for you are not under law but under grace."** That's the truth, the whole truth and nothing but the truth!

Sin thrives in the darkness and in the shadows of secrecy, shame and fear. Freedom flourishes in the light of honest, authentic disclosure to God and trustworthy people. If you have found the humility and courage to share your prayers of confession and surrender in your group, good for you! If you haven't done that yet, what is holding you back?

Let's look at one more Scripture, and then close in prayer.

*Do you not know that when you present yourselves to someone as slaves for obedience, you are slaves of the one whom you obey, either of sin resulting in death, or of obedience resulting in righteousness? But thanks be to God that though you were slaves of sin, you became obedient from the heart to that form of teaching to which you were committed, and having been freed from sin, you became slaves of righteousness... For when you were slaves of sin, you were free in regard to righteousness. Therefore what benefit were you then deriving from the things of which you are now ashamed? For the outcome of those things is death. But now having been freed from sin and enslaved to God, you derive your benefit, resulting in sanctification, and the outcome, eternal life.*

ROMANS 6:16-18; 20-22

There you have it. Your new position *in Christ*:

- Crucified with Christ
- Dead to sin (it no longer has the legal power to force you to do its bidding)
- Buried with Him (Romans 6:4)
- Freed from sin's control
- Raised up with Jesus to walk in a new life... His life! (Romans 6:4)
- Alive to God

## PRAY

*Dear heavenly Father, these are hard truths to really grab hold of because they go so much against the grain of my experience. Failing so many times to try and overcome sin has trained me to believe I am too weak to fight it. I see now that I've been lied to. I've sinned and allowed sin to control my body while all along in Christ I have been dead to sin's control and alive to God. I'm sorry, Lord, for not seeing where I am... in Christ. I now choose to believe that I am crucified with Christ, dead to sin's power and control, and alive to God's power and freedom. I choose to present my entire body to You, Lord, for You to live Your sin-hating, righteousness-loving life in and through me. In the name of Christ, my Rescuer I pray. Amen.*

# why is this Christian life so hard?
## THE FLESH VS. THE SPIRIT

Have you wondered why it is so hard to be a follower of Jesus? If so, welcome to the club. Believe me, you are not the only one who struggles to walk free in Christ. It's easy to look around at people in church and get faked out into thinking everybody else is living life on some sort of higher spiritual plane... that being a "good Christian" just comes naturally to them. Trust me. It doesn't come naturally to anybody. But it does come *supernaturally*.

Is there a power source to help us get... and stay... unstuck? That is the subject of this fourth study.

Before we try and answer the title question, let's briefly look back at the good stuff we've discussed so far. First, let's review our definition of "freedom in Christ" from **Study #1:**

> Freedom in Christ is overcoming sin's power and the devil's lies through repentance and faith in the truth, joyfully living in the fullness of the Holy Spirit as a secure, loved, accepted and significant child of the God of grace.

What we are shooting for in these eight studies is an understanding of how to increasingly experience that kind of freedom. Though, "We all stumble in many ways," (James 3:2), we can always come back to the Lord in confession and repentance and find cleansing and forgiveness (1 John 1:9). And the more we grasp hold of the truth about who Christ is in us and who we are in Christ, the more we find sin loosening its grip on our lives. I hope and pray this kind of freedom is the deep and growing longing of your heart.

In **Study #2** we looked at our identity in Christ, "who we are." We saw that we truly are *a secure, loved, accepted and significant child of the God of grace.* We may not be experiencing it fully right now, but that is not because God doesn't love us. It's because we are still influenced by the "stale coffee grounds" that keep us from fully believing the truth.

**Study #3** taught us that in Christ we are truly dead to sin's demanding, dictatorial control over our lives. No matter how strong sin's pull may seem to our hearts, as God's children we are never in a position where we have to sin. We are alive to God and His new life is continually flowing into our spirit. God desires His new life to flow through our soul (how we think, feel and choose) and into our physical body (what we do). The question is—are we going to allow the parts of our bodies to be used for what is right or what is wrong? If we give in to sin, we are submitting to its slavery in our lives and we get trapped. If we surrender to Christ, we can experience His power that enables us to overcome sin's control.

## THIS IS A CHOICE WE MUST MAKE MANY TIMES EVERY DAY

Despite all the good... and totally true... things that God has accomplished for us, there is still another piece of the puzzle. What is our power source to live free in Christ? What kind of "engine" is under the hood of our spiritual lives and how powerful is it?

©2015 Mike Taylor

Before we tackle that question, the following project should help you see areas of life in which you may be experiencing a supernatural "power shortage."

>> Check any of the examples below that you have recently experienced:

## Supernatural "Power Shortages"

☐ I know that I should get up early and read the Bible to start my day, but it is so hard to get motivated to get up earlier than I already am

☐ Part of me wants to go to the Sunday worship service at church but there's so much to do around the house—plus it's such a beautiful day

☐ I know I ought to turn off the TV and spend time with my spouse or play with the kids, but I'm so tired, and it's a big game (or my favorite show)...

☐ I realize that Christ wants me to keep my cool, but that guy (or girl) at work (or school or on the road...) is driving me crazy and my anger just takes over

☐ There's no good reason why I shouldn't cut back on eating and start exercising more consistently and I know what I need to do to get healthy, but it's so hard to get started

☐ I got caught off guard and didn't know what to do. I know lying is wrong but I was in a really awkward place and I could've looked really bad... maybe even lost my job... if I told the truth

☐ I know that God has promised to supply all my needs, but I worry and fret over finances and I've lost my peace of mind...not to mention some sleep

☐ I heard a sermon on the importance of sharing Christ with those around me, but when I think about witnessing to my neighbor—all kinds of fears and anxieties take over

☐ I see the chores around the house piling up and it's driving me nuts, but I just can't seem to get going

☐ I know the dangers that are only a click away on the internet, but I'm looking for some excitement and I know how to get it. After all, won't God forgive me?

☐ I've seen the destructive effects of alcohol in my life and others' but I still feel a strong pull toward the next drink/hit/pill, and besides... I've got it under control

**>> Hopefully by now you have established some pretty solid trust relationships in your group. Take some time before moving on to share with the group what you checked above, then pray for one another in the areas that were discussed.**

I'm sure you'd be able to make your own list of battles you've been experiencing lately. We all have them, every one of us. But why? If we have such a secure identity in Christ and such a strong position in Christ, why is the Christian life still such a struggle? Where is the power to do what we know is right?

The apostle Paul, despite his unwavering dedication to Christ, knew exactly what we are talking about. His struggle with sin will help shine some light on our struggle with sin. Here's just a snapshot of what he wrote in Romans 7:

>> Go ahead and write in the space below your own version (or paraphrase) of Paul's words in Romans 7:15-18. In your group, read your version and discuss together the questions, "What was Paul's struggle?" "In what way(s) is Paul's and our struggle the same?"

*For what I am doing I do not understand; for I am not practicing what I would like to do, but I am doing the very thing I hate. But if I do the very thing I do not want to do, I agree with the Law [God's Word], confessing that the Law is good. So now, no longer am I the one doing it, but sin which dwells in me. For I know that nothing good dwells in me, that is, in my flesh; for the willing is present in me, but the doing of the good is not.*

ROMANS 7:15-18 *[words in brackets are mine]*

### Paraphrase Paul's Words from Romans 7

_____

_____

_____

_____

_____

_____

Here are some bullet points to sum up Paul's (and our) struggle against sin:

- God's Word is good. I know that in my heart. Ignorance of what is right is not my main problem.

- I know what the right thing to do is.

- Sin still dwells in me as Christ's follower and it has a powerful mind of its own, seeking to control me and push me to do what is wrong.

- There is a part of me called "the flesh" that is attracted to sin.

- My problem boils down to a power shortage. As a Christian, deep down I want to do what's right and pleasing to God, but I don't know how to connect with the power to overcome sin and do what is right. How do I get plugged in?

By the way, you might be wondering what "flesh" refers to. In the Bible, "flesh" can mean different things. It can mean our physical bodies, but that is not the meaning here in Romans 7. Our physical bodies are not evil; in Christ our bodies are the temple of the Holy Spirit (1 Corinthians 6:19). As we saw in our last study, we can choose to use our bodies for good or evil. So the key to overcome sin is certainly not to hate our bodies or physically abuse them.

"Flesh" in this context refers to that inner urge toward self-sufficiency and self-reliance that dwells in all people (Christians included) and which links up with the power of sin in our lives to pressure us to live selfishly and sinfully. Our flesh does not represent our core identity (who we are in Christ as God's children), but it is a very real and active presence in our lives.

I kind of like to view our flesh as the "toxic waste" left over from our B.C. (Before Christ) days, but that definition is off the record. You didn't really hear that from me.

Anyway, there is an internal war in our lives between the "flesh" and the "Spirit," and it is a battle we will face until the day we die. But as hard as it can seem to get the upper hand, this is a battle you can win. At its root, this conflict is a war between "who we were" (apart from Christ) vs. "who we are" (in Christ). In fact, one of the apostle Paul's main appeals to living in the right way is that sinning just isn't "you" anymore... at least not the real, new, core "you" in Christ. See what I mean:

> *Do not lie to one another, since you laid aside the old self with its evil practices, and have put on the new self who is being renewed to a true knowledge according to the image of the One who created him.*
> COLOSSIANS 3:9-10

Did you catch that? Paul is basically saying, "Stop lying. That's the old, obsolete, dead and gone "you" and you've already had a funeral for that old sinful mess and buried it in the ground. Live life in the new way because the new you now has new life!" And this truth not only applies to "lying" but to every other habit pattern of sin that we struggle with.

We used to "wear" the dirty, smelly, filthy clothes of sin, but now we can "wear" the clean, fresh, bright white clothes of doing what's right. It's kind of like we have two closets now... one with the old, rotten clothes and the other with the new, fresh clothes. We can choose to get our "clothes" for the day out of either closet. It is our choice.

It makes all the sense in the world that we should be able to behave as the new creation in Christ we are (2 Corinthians 5:17). But this is easier said than done. After all, those old clothes might be smelly, but at least they are familiar. Those new clothes might be clean, but we are not so used to them. It can be a real struggle to live as one who has put off the old self and put on the new self, especially when we experience one or more of the following conditions:

**B**oredom

**L**oneliness

**A**nxiety

**S**tress in finances

**T**ension in relationships

**E**xcessive weariness

**D**iscouragement

©2015 Mike Taylor

**» Have you ever found yourself BLASTED, being overwhelmed by an attraction to sin when you experienced any of these seven conditions? Discuss with your group the conditions of your soul that make you particularly vulnerable to giving in to the temptations of sin.**

We have spent considerable time in these studies so far talking about our new and true identity, who we are in Christ. And knowing who we are as God's children is absolutely essential to experiencing our freedom. But it is not enough for you to understand who you are in Christ. Paul understood that better than we do. Remember, he wrote Romans 6 about being dead to sin and alive to God, but then he turned around and struggled terribly in Romans 7! In fact, he closed off that section of his letter by crying out, *"Wretched man that I am! Who will set me free from the body of this death?" (v. 24).*

Notice that Paul didn't say "Wicked man that I am!" He said *"Wretched* man that I am!" Wretched means miserable, and there is probably no more miserable person on earth than the one who knows what is the right thing to do and yet is powerless to do it.

*That's how most Christians live their lives. They are not being successful at connecting with God's power source over sin. Maybe that is how you are living your life today.*

Notice also that Paul did not ask "What will set me free...?" He asked, "Who will set me free...?"

*That's the right question!*

Religion can't set you free. Trying harder won't get you unstuck. Neither will the most earnest spiritual disciplines enable you to escape sin's traps. Only Christ's Spirit can set us free from the power of sin because God alone is more powerful than sin.

*No, knowing who you are in Christ is not enough to win this battle (though power over sin is not possible if you don't know who you are!).*

## YOU MUST ALSO KNOW WHO CHRIST IS IN YOU!

>> Take a minute and jot down adjectives that you would use to describe Jesus Christ. Share your ideas with your group, writing down other good thoughts the group members come up with.

_____

_____

_____

_____

_____

_____

For us to walk in freedom, we must know who Christ is in us, and He is not some wimpy, stringy-haired, pale-faced, string bean who tries to be nice to everybody. Maybe we should all agree together to get rid of every painting or picture of Jesus that makes Him look that way. We could start with the one depicted in the next cartoon.

## Jesus Christ is...

**Immanuel (God with us)**

MATTHEW 1:23

**King of all kings and Lord of all Lords**

REVELATION 19:16

**Lord God, the Almighty, King of the Nations**

REVELATION 15:3

**A victorious Warrior**

ZEPHANIAH 3:17

**The Alpha and Omega, First and Last who conquered death**

REVELATION 1:8,17,18

**The Creator of all things**

COLOSSIANS 1:16

**The One that holds all things together**

COLOSSIANS 1:17

...and more!

And this invincible, sin-squashing, devil-defeating King lives in you and me!

©2015 Mike Taylor

Were we left alone to try and fight sin, we would lose every time. But God has given us an energy source that can enable us to be *joyfully living in the fullness of the Holy Spirit* as our definition of "freedom in Christ" describes. Galatians 5:16-17 teaches:

*But I say, walk by the Spirit, and you will not carry out the desire of the flesh. For the flesh sets its desire against the Spirit, and the Spirit against the flesh; for these are in opposition to one another, so that you may not do the things that you please.*
GALATIANS 5:16-17

You may be tempted to think that Galatians 5:16-17 is describing a tug-o-war match between two equal and opposite powers... the flesh vs. the Spirit with you being the rope! It can certainly feel that way at times. But sin is no match for the Spirit, and neither is our flesh. The Holy Spirit is the Lord. He is Almighty God. Your flesh, even energized by the power of sin, is nothing by comparison.

Now, it's possible that you might be a little confused at this point, because the Galatians 5:16,17 passage talked about "the Spirit" being the One that enables you to keep from walking according to the flesh, not Christ. Don't worry.

Everything that Jesus is in terms of His character, power, greatness and goodness, the Holy Spirit is, too. The Holy Spirit is the Spirit of Christ. In realty, it is the same thing to say that the "Spirit" or the "Spirit of God" or the "Spirit of Christ" or even "Christ" dwells in you (see Romans 8:9,10). In essence and nature, the Holy Spirit is identical to Jesus Christ. The Spirit, however, does not have a physical body as Jesus does, but that's good news. Because the Holy Spirit is spirit, He can live inside your physical body!

The presence and power of the Holy Spirit is essential to our freedom. Paul wrote:

*Now the Lord is the Spirit, and where the Spirit of the Lord is, there is liberty.*
2 CORINTHIANS 3:17

Listen to the power available to us over the flesh and sin through the Holy Spirit:

---

*But if the Spirit of Him who raised Jesus from the dead dwells in you, [and Romans 8:9 tells us that all Christians have the Holy Spirit] He who raised Christ Jesus from the dead will also give life to your mortal bodies through His Spirit who dwells in you. So then, brethren, we are under obligation, not to the flesh, to live according to the flesh– for if you are living according to the flesh, you must die; but if by the Spirit you are putting to death the deeds of the body, you will live.*

ROMANS 8:11-13 *[words in brackets are mine]*

---

Are you beginning to get a picture of the super power that is "under the hood" of your life? Take another look from Ephesians 3:20,21:

---

*Now to Him who is able to do far more abundantly beyond all that we ask or think, according to the power that works within us, to Him be the glory in the church and in Christ Jesus to all generations forever and ever. Amen.*

EPHESIANS 3:20-21

---

The devil wants you to think sin has your number; that you are a loser; that you can't win. He's a liar. God says you have His super power through the Holy Spirit inside you, and He can do incredibly more than you can imagine.

### Who are you going to believe?

Do you now have a greater appreciation for the incredible power to overcome temptation and sin that lives inside of you? You are dead to sin and alive to God because you are in **Christ**. And you have the greatest power in the universe to say "NO!" to sin today and "YES!" to God because **Christ's Spirit is in you!**

>> **As a closing exercise today, in your group, look at the areas of sin you checked earlier in this study and ask God together, through the power of the Holy Spirit within you, to strengthen you to turn away from those sins and instead demonstrate the love, joy, peace, patience, kindness, goodness, faithfulness, gentleness and self-control of the Spirit (Galatians 5:22,23).**

In conclusion, below I have written a personalized version of Paul's prayer at the end of Ephesians 3 for you to pray. It is a prayer to relinquish control of your life to God and to invite the Holy Spirit who is inside you to take over. There can only be one person "behind the wheel" of your life... God or you. If you surrender to God and let Him take the wheel, the engine of the supernatural power of the Holy Spirit is revved up to give energy to your life. If you refuse to give the wheel over to God, you end up behind the car pushing it up the hills of life. Your call...

## PRAY

For this reason, heavenly Father, I kneel before You and ask that You would give me the ability, because of Your great and glorious treasures, to be made strong with power through Your Spirit deep down inside me. By faith, I want Christ to be fully alive and at home in my heart. I know that I am already rooted and grounded in Your love, but I want to understand, with all God's people, how broad, long, high and deep Your love is, and to really know Your love deep down inside, so that it is far beyond mere head knowledge. In that way I can be filled up to all Your fullness. I now praise You, Lord, for You are able to do way more than all that I can ask or even imagine, according to this mighty resurrection power of the Holy Spirit that works within me. To You be all the glory in the church and in Christ Jesus to all people everywhere for all time. Amen.

# when life is a pain
## MOVING BEYOND DISTRUST

There are some voices within the world of Christianity today that are preaching a "gospel" that sounds something like this: *Come to Jesus, and if you really live for Him, all the good things in life that you have always wanted will be yours, and all the bad stuff in life you have never wanted, won't be yours.* Or something to that effect.

Generally, the underlying belief in that message is that good health and good fortune are somehow wrapped up in the package that Christ purchased for us on the cross. The implication is that if you are not experiencing this quality of life now, there is something seriously lacking in your understanding of how to live out your faith in Jesus.

This kind of teaching can sound really convincing when it comes from the mouth of a handsome, healthy, eloquent, energetic... and wealthy... preacher in a well-tailored suit, holding court in an expensive, expansive building. After all, look at how it has "worked" for him! And, of course, such a message is extremely inviting to those envious of the "good life" or just plain down on their luck.

However, for something to be true according to what God says is true, it must be true for all people in all places. It has to be true in the slums of urban India as well as in the subdivisions of suburban America. It must not only be real and relevant for white-collar businessmen in the West; it must radically impact the lives of war-torn refugees in the Middle East or Africa.

In my opinion, the reason this distorted teaching has flourished in our country is that we don't "do pain" very well in America. We feel very entitled to a healthy, wealthy, pain-free and suffering-free life. Our bodies hurt, and there are a hundred different pills we can take to get rid of the pain. Our souls hurt and so we expect there to be a prescription to make us feel all better in that way, too. But all we end up doing is numbing the pain.

Now don't get me wrong. If there is a legitimate medical means to alleviate suffering, I'm all for it. But it is neither wise nor healthy to avoid facing the root problems of our souls by self-medicating with some legal or illegal substance.

**How does this issue come into play in our search for "freedom in Christ"?**

Good question! When it comes to the subject of freedom, it would be easy to buy into "prosperity preaching" and fall prey to the lie that says "Christianity means freedom from pain and suffering."

Actually, nothing could be further from the truth. Even a quick glance at Scripture will tell you that such freedom only comes when we graduate to heaven and spend the rest of forever with Jesus. What we can experience this side of heaven, however, is freedom *in the midst of suffering*, and that is the subject of this fifth study.

I think this would be a good place to pray...

*Father in heaven, Jesus was called a man of sorrows and acquainted with grief. His life was not miraculously shielded from pain. In fact, the Bible says that He learned obedience through what He suffered (Hebrews 5:8). So how could we ever think our lives would be different? Jesus also had very little in material possessions. The same was true of the apostle Paul, who seemed to be a magnet for suffering of almost every kind. So if pain is inevitable and suffering is unavoidable, and yet Jesus experienced perfect freedom, and even Paul lived a life of great liberty, how can we, too, discover freedom in the midst of such a painful world as this? I ask You to open my eyes and my heart to the truth, in Jesus' name. Amen.*

It would be helpful to state at this point, I think, that there is *absolutely nothing or no one in this world that can ultimately keep you from experiencing freedom...* aside from you and your own decisions.

## YOU CAN CHOOSE TO LIVE A FREE LIFE, NO MATTER WHAT THIS MESSED UP WORLD MAY THROW AT YOU.

Now that's a truth that is worth remembering. It is a truth that should bring hope.

But there is a critical issue that we need to face before we can enter into that kind of unshakable victory and freedom.

**>> The critical issue we need to face relates to God Himself. We need to wrestle with the question: What part does God play when it comes to the pain and suffering in life? Does He cause our suffering? Is He to blame? Take a crack at answering these questions in the blank space below. Be honest in expressing your thoughts and feelings. Then discuss your answer with your group.**

_____

_____

_____

_____

_____

_____

_____

_____

_____

_____

Bible scholars and godly men have wrestled with these questions for ages: *Is God good? If God is good, why doesn't He rush in and stop suffering? Is it because He is not able to do so? Is God good but not great (all powerful)? Is He able to stop suffering but chooses not to for some reason? Does He really care about how much life hurts?*

Maybe you have struggled with these questions yourself. Perhaps you have suffered horrible abuse in your life, and you cried out to God for help and all you heard was silence. Maybe you are going through a really rough time right now. Finances are a constant headache and heartache; debt threatens to sweep over you like a tsunami. Or relationships are explosive, toxic or just painful. Or health problems are chronic or acute and are eroding any joy and hope you once had.

It could very well be you are experiencing these things yourself. Or maybe you are watching a loved one go through them... which is often harder.

Maybe you are watching your career or reputation systematically skewered by the envy, spite or bitterness of others. Perhaps you are terrorized by anxiety or fear of what might happen to you or someone you love, or you find yourself swirling down into a black hole of depression and you wonder, *"Where is God?"*

If any of these things... or any other equally painful experience... is yours, you are not alone. It may be surprising to you that many godly people throughout history have felt the same things, and God was not ashamed to put what they wrote into the Bible. Here's a brief sampling of what they felt and experienced, and how they got through it.

**»** Go ahead and circle any of the thoughts, emotions or conditions expressed in the Scriptures below that echo what you have experienced, or are experiencing now.

---

*My tears have been my food day and night, while they say to me all day long, "Where is your God?" These things I remember and I pour out my soul within me. For I used to go along with the throng and lead them in procession to the house of God, with the voice of joy and thanksgiving, a multitude keeping festival. Why are you in despair, O my soul? And why have you become disturbed within me? Hope in God, for I shall again praise Him for the help of His presence. O my God, my soul is in despair within me; therefore I remember You...*

PSALM 42:3-6A

*My eyes run down with streams of water because of the destruction of the daughter of my people. My eyes pour down unceasingly, without stopping, until the Lord looks down and sees from heaven. My eyes bring pain to my soul because of all the daughters of my city. My enemies without cause hunted me down like a bird; they have silenced me in the pit and have placed a stone on me. Waters flowed over my head; I said, "I am cut off!" I called on Your name, O Lord, out of the lowest pit. You have heard my voice, "Do not hide Your ear from my prayer for relief; from my cry for help." You drew near when I called on You. You said, "Do not fear!"*

LAMENTATIONS 3:48-57

---

Weeping. Unceasing grief. Humiliation. Despair. Depression. Terror. Panic.

## PEACE. COMFORT. RELIEF. HELP.

**»** Have you ever expressed such raw emotion and deep need to God? Think of a time when you were desperate and called out to God for help (maybe today?). Take some time and talk about that incident(s) with your group. Did you sense the "help of His presence" like the writer of Psalm 42? (By the way, if you have to answer "no" to that last question, don't be afraid to say that and to talk about how alone or angry that made you feel with those in your group.)

Jesus said that in this world we will have trouble (John 16:33). If Jesus says it's going to happen, count on it. But He also said that He would give us His special brand of peace... not the world's peace that only comes when things are easy...

but peace even when all hell is breaking loose. It is the peace that overcomes anxiety and fear *in the midst of the storm*, even when everyone else around you is going nuts (see John 14:27). It is the kind of peace that acts like a military garrison, protecting your heart and mind in the darkest, most turbulent times (Philippians 4:6,7).

*Think about it.*

*Isn't it true that you can go through just about anything if you have peace of mind and heart?*

So here's a crucial question:

**»** **What can we count on God to do for us when we cry out to Him in our distress? Take some time in your group to try and answer that question.**

**What conclusions did your group come to? Go ahead and jot them down below.**

_____

_____

_____

_____

_____

_____

True, there are times when God miraculously heals or directly intervenes to change circumstances for the better in order to show people how powerful He is. And we ought to pray, asking God to act in that way. He certainly can do miracles and supernaturally heal in response to our prayers. And sometimes He does just that.

*But what about the times when He doesn't...?*

Many times it seems like God has a different plan.

After being given an amazing privilege by God to see something other mortals had never seen, the apostle Paul was struck by some terrible physical ailment brought on by Satan (and, incidentally, permitted by God). Paul prayed three times that it would leave him. But God, in His wisdom and mercy, chose not to answer Paul's prayer for healing. God knew that the miserable affliction... whatever it was... was somehow necessary for Paul's spiritual health.

Here is Paul's account of that situation, including how he responded to God's plan for him:

> *Because of the surpassing greatness of the revelations, for this reason, to keep me from exalting myself, there was given me a thorn in the flesh, a messenger of Satan to torment me– to keep me from exalting myself! Concerning this, I implored the Lord three times that it might leave me. And He has said to me, 'My grace is sufficient for you, for power is perfected in weakness.' Most gladly, therefore, I will rather boast about my weaknesses, so that the power of Christ may dwell in me. Therefore, I am well content with weaknesses, with insults, with distresses, with persecutions, with difficulties, for Christ's sake; for when I am weak, then I am strong.*
> 2 CORINTHIANS 12:7-10

What conclusions can we come to in light of what Paul experienced and wrote about?

- *God's grace—His enabling power to live life and endure hardship in the way God wants us to—is enough... no matter how hard things get.*

- *God sometimes sees fit to sacrifice our temporary experience of pleasure, health, and prosperity in order to do a deeper, more lasting work in our hearts.*

**>> How do those two statements I just made grab you? Do you agree? Do you think it's fair for God to act that way? Do you think it's a "good deal" or would you rather God just leave you alone to enjoy life? Take a few minutes and discuss these questions in your group.**

From Paul's experience, it is clear we cannot put our ultimate hope in the cessation of tough times... at least not this side of heaven. That may not be what you want to hear, but it is reality. Pain and suffering can fill our days with great loneliness, fear, anxiety and grief. So what can we count on God to provide? I think the following Scripture gives a clear answer to that question:

*Do not fear, for I am with you; do not anxiously look about you, for I am your God. I will strengthen you, surely I will help you, surely I will uphold you with My righteous right hand.*
ISAIAH 41:10

**Here is what we can glean from this great Bible verse:**

- Fear and anxiety about the present and future do not need to control us
- The antidote for fear and anxiety is an awareness of God's presence
- Since He is God, He can be with us at every moment in every place
- God promises to be with us in a very active way that will make a big difference
- God promises to help us and hold us up, even when we can't feel Him
- God will personally, directly hold us up with His hand of authority and power, doing what is right on our behalf

Here is another portion of the Bible that should help us see that we are not doomed to a life of anxiety and fear about the present and future:

> *Blessed is the man who trusts in the Lord and whose trust is the Lord. For he will be like a tree planted by the water, that extends its roots by a stream and will not fear when the heat comes; but its leaves will be green, and it will not be anxious in a year of drought nor cease to yield fruit.*
> JEREMIAH 17:7-8

**»** In the table below, rate yourself in terms of how you typically respond "when the heat is on." For example, do you experience the freedom that comes from knowing "the help of His presence" or are you fearful and anxious? Be honest and put an "x" where you think you most often land emotionally in these times of stress. Then, discuss your answers in your group and talk about how a clearer, fuller, truer understanding of who God is can help move you along the scale to the right.

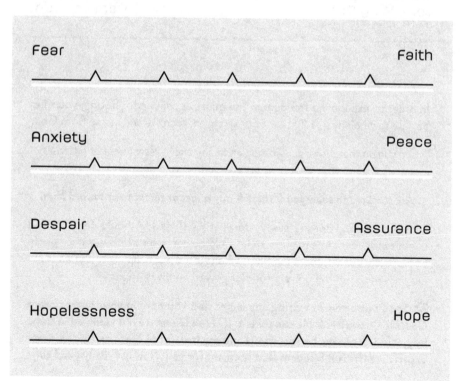

Fear — Faith

Anxiety — Peace

Despair — Assurance

Hopelessness — Hope

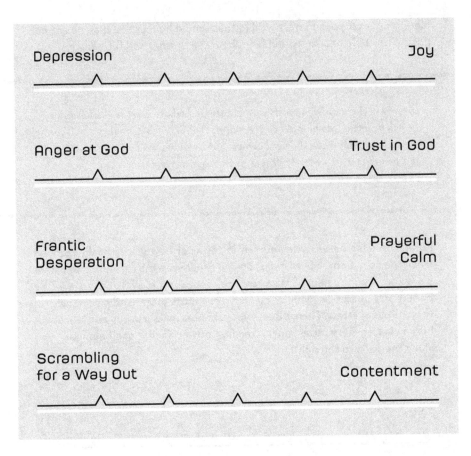

In order to experience freedom in the midst of pain and suffering, you must be able to wholeheartedly seek your strength, security and peace from God.

*Can you do that or are you holding on to any anger, resentment or bitterness toward God?*

**Ask the Lord to show you if there is any anger or resentment toward Him.**

Let's face it, God doesn't always do what we think He should do. And God doesn't always act in a manner that would be consistent with our choices. To be perfectly honest, there are times when we are not happy with the way God has chosen to run the universe and/or govern our lives. Right?

**》 Spell out below in writing any anger that you have in your heart toward God. Don't be afraid. He can take it. If these issues are not resolved in some way, you will always be suspicious and mistrustful of Him, and you'll never experience the full freedom that is meant for you. Now is a really good time**

**to express what you are feeling. After writing it down, talk about it in your group. And pray for each other. This could be a very liberating time for you.**

_____

_____

_____

_____

_____

_____

_____

_____

_____

Before wrapping up this study with some final thoughts and a prayer, here are a couple more passages of the Bible that are very relevant to our discussion.

*Seek the Lord while He may be found; call upon Him while He is near. Let the wicked forsake his way and the unrighteous man his thoughts, and let him return to the Lord, and He will have compassion on him, and to our God for He will abundantly pardon. "For My thoughts are not your thoughts, nor are your ways My ways," declares the Lord. "For as the heavens are higher than the earth, so are My ways higher than your ways and My thoughts than your thoughts."*

ISAIAH 55:6-9

Since God's ways and thoughts are so much higher (wiser and better) than ours, it is important that we learn to clearly hear what He is saying and see what He is doing. Before we can do that well, we have to give up our own flawed and sinful ideas and plans. That's easier said than done, we realize.

This is serious stuff and we need to shoot straight and talk straight about some things. And we will do that in just a minute. But before we do, we thought you'd enjoy a quick breather and chuckle from a cartoon that pokes fun at how easy it can be to totally miss what God is trying to tell us.

And we know that God causes all things to work together for good to those who love God, to those who are called according to His purpose. For those whom He foreknew, He also predestined to become conformed to the image of His Son, so that He would be the firstborn among many brethren; and those whom He predestined, He also called; and these whom He called, He also justified; and these whom He justified, He also glorified. What then shall we say to these things? If God is for us, who is against us? He who did not spare His own Son, but delivered Him over for us all, how will He not also with Him freely give us all things?

ROMANS 8:28-32

There are some very important truths we need to take away from these two sections of the Bible:

- *God is very kind and compassionate and is always ready to forgive you when you turn away from evil and come back to Him.*

- *There is no time to waste; you should come back to Him right now while you can!*

- *No matter how smart you think you are or how right you think your way of doing things is, God is infinitely smarter than you are and His ways are vastly better than yours.*

- *Since God's thoughts and ways are so much higher than yours, you should not be surprised when He handles things differently from how you think He will or should.*

- *Though bad things do happen and likely have happened to you, God can and will bring good out of them if you love Him and are called by Him for His great purposes.*

- *God's great purpose is to chip away the rough edges in your life and make you more like Jesus.*

- *God is for you if you are His child; He is on your side*

- *Since God is for you, it really doesn't matter who is against you because God cannot be stopped.*

- *If God through Jesus loved you enough to take your place on the cross, can't He be trusted to take care of you in all areas of your life?*

So where does that leave you? In our next study we will talk about how to resolve your anger toward others and toward yourself. But right now you may have a rather large hurdle to overcome... your anger toward God.

In order to be free from anger, resentment and bitterness toward God—you have to take the path of humility. Though it may seem like He has done so, God has never wronged you. He can't because He is good. He always has been good and always will be good. Many times we accuse God of being unfair, unjust, uncaring, unkind, uninvolved, unfeeling, weak, cold, passive, distant or even mean, cruel or abusive.

### *He is not any of those things.*

Sometimes it is really hard to admit that we have been wrong about God and to humble ourselves and put our trust in Him. We have so many "Why?" questions. And I really believe God would answer every one of them if we were able to understand His answers. One day we will understand—when we see Him face to face.

Until then, you might want to consider finding a box and writing down all the "Why?" questions you have for God. Put them in the box, not to be forgotten, but to be reserved until the day... perhaps in heaven... when Jesus Himself will open that box and answer them all to your deepest satisfaction.

**>>** One more time of discussion with your group should really be helpful to you. Would you be courageous and honest enough to pull out one or two of your "Why? Box" questions and read it/them to your group? Then pray for each other that you'd be able to release any anger you still have toward God and find the grace and freedom to truly trust Him.

God's Word, the Bible says:

*The Lord is righteous in all His ways and kind in all His deeds.*
PSALM 145:17

Are you able to say, "Yes Lord, I believe that is true"? Will you take a moment and thank God for being right and kind in what He does and how He does it?

God's Word also says:

> **The Lord is near to all who call upon Him, to all who call upon Him in truth.**
> PSALM 145:18

The Lord is waiting to draw near to you, if you will let Him. He is a gracious, merciful and compassionate God.

If you have struggled with letting go of your anger toward God, it may take a little while to move beyond distrust to true faith in Him. Take your time. Let our closing prayer be a beginning point to gently nudge you forward into your own honest, open, real time of talking things over with God.

## PRAY

*Dear heavenly Father, it is so easy to run You through the filter of my own pain and come out the other side with a picture of You that is not someone I like or trust at all. And, if Your Word is indeed truth, that image of You is not a true picture of who You are. I am sorry for judging You according to my ways and thoughts and, in my pride, believing I was right and justified for holding on to my anger and even hatred of You. I humble myself now before You and admit that as the sky is vastly higher than this ground on which I stand, so are Your ways and thoughts more vast and magnificently higher than mine. I now confess I have been unfairly resentful and bitter toward You. (This would be a good place to get specific with God regarding the reasons you have been angry with Him.)*

*I choose to thank You that no matter how awful things have been in my life, You are able to turn those things into good for me by making me more like Jesus. I wish You had an easier way to do it, but I choose to let the endurance You are building in my life make me fully mature in Christ. I choose to trust You now and wait for the day in heaven when You will explain all the questions in my "Why? Box." Although I have felt alone, I know now that I have never been abandoned by You. One day I will be able to celebrate with all the saints around the world who have experienced the same kinds of sufferings that I have. And I will be able to testify, just like they will, that after suffering for a little while You, the God of all grace, who has called me to Your eternal glory in Christ, did indeed perfect, confirm, strengthen and establish me. To You be all authority forever and ever. (1 Peter 5:9-11). Amen.*

# the great challenge of freedom

## EXTENDING FORGIVENESS

It is one thing... and a very important thing... to resolve our issues of anger toward God. It is another thing to face the pain we feel due to the hurts that people (including ourselves) have brought into our lives. In our years of working with believers through Freedom in Christ Ministries, perhaps we have found no more crucial issue than this one.

We have also seen defeated, discouraged, disillusioned Christians who were convinced that God was distant and disinterested in their lives—suddenly catch fire for God. Mourning turned to dancing. Sorrow to joy. Spiritual lukewarmness to spiritual passion.

*What was the cause of such a turnaround?*

Many times it was coming to the point of deep, heartfelt forgiveness. This issue may very well be the pivotal point in your spiritual life as well, and so it is the subject of this sixth study.

*Will you join me in this prayer?*

*Dear Father, the good news of the "good news" of Jesus is that through Him we are forgiven of all our sins. That is not anything I deserved, and yet You gave that to me anyway. However, when I think of what has been done to me in the past and* that You would expect me to forgive those who have hurt me, that doesn't sound like particularly good news. I'm not sure I want to, or even should do that. Open my eyes to what forgiveness is and what it isn't so that I can be free from my anger, resentment and bitterness toward those who have hurt me... even if the main person I have been angry with is me. Amen.

>> I would imagine that most followers of Jesus have an intuitive sense that extending forgiveness to others is something that Christians are supposed to do. But what does it mean to forgive someone? And why is forgiveness important? Write down your thoughts below and discuss your answers in the group.

_____

_____

_____

_____

_____

_____

_____

_____

_____

_____

As we begin this study, it would be good to nail down the truth that forgiveness is indeed something that God wants us to extend to others. Let's take a look at a couple of Bible verses:

Let all bitterness and wrath and anger and clamor and slander be put away from you, along with all malice. Be kind to one another, tender-hearted, forgiving each other, just as God in Christ also has forgiven you.
EPHESIANS 4:31-32

> *So, as those who have been chosen of God, holy and beloved, put on a heart of compassion, kindness, humility, gentleness and patience; bearing with one another, and forgiving each other, whoever has a complaint against anyone; just as the Lord forgave you, so also should you.*
>
> COLOSSIANS 3:12-13

Any doubts remaining that forgiveness is not just a nice idea, but something that God requires and expects of us?

Before we move on, some explanation of those two passages from the Bible will be helpful:

- The verses in Ephesians tell us to put away all anger from us. You could get the wrong impression that all anger is wrong. Not so. In fact, in verse 26 of that same chapter it says, "Be angry, but don't sin." Anger is a normal human emotion and should be our reaction to injustice. How do you "be angry, but don't sin"? That is an important question because verse 27 warns us not to "let the sun go down on your anger and do not give the devil an opportunity [base of operations]."

  What does that mean? Well, it would be silly to interpret verse 27 legalistically. I mean, suppose sunset today was at 7:35 pm and at 7:34 pm you hung up the phone after somebody called you and swore at you like a sailor, calling you every profane name in the book. That Bible verse doesn't mean that you have exactly 60 seconds to deal with your anger or the devil will get you!

  Letting the sun go down on our anger involves our tendency to stuff it down inside... which isn't particularly good for your blood pressure or stomach ulcers. It can also involve letting it fester or boil over so that it scalds others.

The sad results of anger out of control are harsh words, violence, vengeance, division, marriage breakups, church splits and civil wars. That's why we need to "put away" those things that Ephesians 4:31,32 talks about.

- As Colossians 3 tells us, God has chosen us. We are holy (set apart from sin to Him) and dearly loved by Him. Our new identity in Christ enables us to "put on a heart of compassion... forgiving each other." Because God has dealt kindly and forgivingly with us we can, and need to, treat others in the same way.

- Notice also in the Colossians 3 verses that there are no exceptions to the mandate to forgive. Whoever (that's you) has a complaint (that's anything that you don't like) against anyone (that's the rest of the human race), we are to forgive. That's pretty comprehensive.

>> In your group, talk about what the Lord has forgiven you from. Sometimes we forget. It's good to remember how merciful and gracious God has been to us; it humbles us and helps foster a forgiving spirit in us toward other people.

By now, you've probably figured out where I'm headed in this study. I hope you go with me. Our destination? Coming to the point where you'll have opportunity to begin the process of forgiving those who have hurt you. But before we come to that place, there are some more issues we need to examine first. I'll use a Q&A format to do that.

*Feel free to use any of the questions below as launching points for discussion in your group.*

## >> What exactly does it mean to forgive someone? Does that mean somehow that I magically forget what was done to me?

When you combine the three words in the Bible translated "forgive" from the original language into English you get this definition: "to give an undeserved gift of releasing someone from obligation to you by canceling the debt they owe you." Matthew 6:12 and Matthew 18:23-35 make that clear. In other words you let them off the hook, even though they don't deserve it.

The idea is that someone owes us something and we make the choice to erase it from "the debit column" in our accounting of their relationship to us. We choose to no longer "make them pay" for what they did, even though in a sense "they owe us."

Or you could look at it this way: It's like we realize we have all this nasty, smelly trash of unforgiveness in the "house of our soul" and we deliberately carry it out to the curb, allowing God to take it away from us forever.

©Mike Taylor 2015

Once you make the choice to truly forgive someone for what they did or didn't do, the memory may or may not fade over time. But to wait until we forget all our pain before we make the choice to forgive would be a mistake, because we don't begin to heal from the hurt until we first make the choice to forgive.

## FORGIVENESS PRECEDES AND IS THE PREREQUISITE FOR GENUINE HEALING.

**>> How can you expect me to forgive? You don't know what this person did to me and you have no idea how much this hurts!**

You are right. I don't know. But God does and He is the One that is calling you to forgive. I don't say that to be harsh, but simply to tell you the truth. God is not asking you to do the impossible. By His strength and grace you can make the choice to forgive, but you can't do it on your own.

God is moving you toward forgiveness because He loves you. He wants you to be free from the pain of your past. When you hold on to your bitterness and unforgiveness, you may think you are protecting yourself from future pain, but you are preventing yourself from healing. Let God into those wounded places so that you can heal. You do that by making the choice to forgive. Time does not heal all wounds; only God does. Again, forgiveness comes first.

**>> Note: If you have not already paused to discuss any of these questions in your group, this would be a good place to stop. Talk about what has been done to you in the past that is really hard to let go of. Maybe it is something that you did and you are having a really hard time letting yourself off the hook. Getting these things out and talking about them might be the first step toward truly being free. Don't miss this chance to bring out into the light something that maybe you have hidden or tried to forget about for a long time.**

**>> How can I forgive this person? There's no way to contact them. Plus they never asked for forgiveness...**

It is easy to confuse forgiveness with reconciliation. Reconciliation is becoming friends again with people we had become estranged from. Whenever it is possible and safe to do so, this is a worthy pursuit. (It would not be safe to seek reconciliation, however, with someone that could still harm or abuse you). But forgiveness is different. Reconciliation takes "two to tango." Forgiveness, however, is something you do in the presence of God without the other person needing to be there. Sometimes the person we need to forgive is totally gone from our life. That doesn't matter. We can and still need to forgive them.

An important thing to remember is that we are not exempted from needing to forgive someone if they don't apologize. Jesus is our example. He said, "Father, forgive them for they don't know what they are doing" even while they were crucifying Him (see Luke 23:34). In the same way Stephen forgave those who were stoning him (Acts 7:60). In neither case were the perpetrators of evil apologizing.

>> **If I forgive this person, that means they'll get off scot-free! They deserve to be punished for what they did!**

This is a tough one, I know, but there is an answer to this complaint. First of all, when you forgive someone you are giving up the right to seek revenge and "make them pay." Though you remove yourself from the picture of punishing them, they still have to deal with God Himself. Romans 12:19-21 warns us against trying to extract our "pound of flesh" and gives us another way... Christ's way... to treat those who sin against us:

*Never take your own revenge, beloved, but leave room for the wrath of God, for it is written, "Vengeance is Mine, I will repay," says the Lord. "But if your enemy is hungry, feed him, and if he is thirsty, give him a drink; for in so doing you will heap burning coals on his head." Do not be overcome by evil, but overcome evil with good.*
ROMANS 12:19-21

God wants us to learn to love our enemies (Matthew 5:44) and not lie awake longing for the day when God zaps them. That was Jonah's problem and you can read all about it in the Old Testament book named after him. He was a mess.

God may choose to move in tender grace and mercy toward the person who wronged you. After all that's what He did with you, after you wronged Him with your sins. Right? You and I deserved to be punished for our sins, but God forgave us. That is called mercy and we need to exercise that godly quality toward those who have sinned against us.

If it turns out that the person who hurt you travels the whole course of their life without repentance toward God and faith in our Lord Jesus, then vengeance from God is what they will experience. But that is God's job and is never to come from us.

Right now you could still be experiencing the painful consequences of someone's sin against you. The harsh reality of life on a sinful planet is that you could very well suffer those consequences at some level for the rest of your life. That is a choice you would never have made; it just happened. The choice you do have, however, is whether you will experience those painful consequences in the bondage of bitterness or in the freedom of forgiveness. That choice is yours.

**>> What about forgiving myself? I've screwed up my life really bad and hold a lot of things against myself. What do I do?**

Forgiving oneself is a huge issue for a lot of people. Many are quick to forgive others but are just as quick to keep beating themselves up over past sins and mistakes. Satan, the accuser of the brethren, wants you and me to believe that it is good, noble and justified to punish ourselves. It is not. Jesus said on the cross, "It is finished!" or literally "Paid in full!" What He meant was that the total 100% punishment and payment for all the sins of all mankind for all history was completed... by Him... not by you. That is *grace*!

And so, when you beat yourself up for your sins you are basically saying, "Lord, I don't think You suffered enough for me. I must also suffer for my sins." Do you see how you are actually calling Jesus a liar if you punish yourself (or others) when Christ has declared His punishment for you (and them) complete?

So, forgiving yourself is simply accepting the truth that Christ's shed blood and death on the cross was the full and sufficient payment for your sins, too. You can let yourself off the hook, because God through Christ has let you off the hook already. It's over.

Romans 8:1 (ESV) says, "There is therefore now no condemnation for those who are in Christ Jesus." Now means *now*. No means *no*!

Won't you fully receive God's pardon today? Today could finally be the end of your guilt and shame as you accept the truth that God has cast all your sins into the depths of the sea (Micah 7:19). And though your sins were once like scarlet, they are now as white as snow (Isaiah 1:18).

**>> Here is another really good place to stop and talk in your group. Discuss whether it has been hard for you to forgive yourself. If so, why? Talk about what the following verses mean for you today: "[God] then says, 'And their sins and their lawless deeds I will remember no more.' Now where there is forgiveness of these things, there is no longer any offering for sin" (Hebrews 10:17, 18).**

## A Life-Transforming Exercise

As we conclude this sixth study, I will be leading you through a process that will provide the opportunity to forgive those (including yourself) that have hurt you. Take your time. Don't rush through this experience. Give God ample opportunity to speak to you and take the time with Him to be real about how you feel as you process through your pain.

**First,** we certainly want to bring God into the picture from the start by asking

Him to show you all the people you need to forgive. You may think you know, but God knows better. Let's pray:

*Dear heavenly Father, nothing is hidden from Your sight. All things are open and laid bare before Your holy eyes. You see with absolute clarity into my heart. Who are the people that I am still holding things against? Please show me who they are. Do I need to forgive myself for anything? I am asking these things because I know I need to forgive, and that is what I intend to do. But I can't do it on my own. I need Your strength, courage, humility, grace, mercy and perseverance to forgive the people You show me. I look forward to the freedom I will gain as You cleanse my soul from the sins of bitterness and unforgiveness. I choose now... in advance... to forgive all these people, including myself, from my heart. In Jesus' name I pray. Amen.*

**Second,** take some time to quietly wait on God as He brings people to mind. You have just asked Him in prayer to do that; don't be surprised when He does. On a separate sheet of paper, write down their names (first names should be enough). Recognize that the people closest to you (parents, spouse, children, siblings, friends, co-workers, fellow church members, etc.) have the greatest capacity to hurt you. Don't bypass writing down anyone's name for fear of dishonoring them. If the Lord brings a memory or name to mind, jot it down. He is answering your prayer for His guidance. Don't forget to write down your own name, if needed.

**Third,** now that you have names written down, allow the Lord to bring specific memories to mind for each person on the list. Some people find it helpful to write down at least a summary of those memories. For some people on your list, there will be numerous things to forgive; for others maybe only one or two things will come to mind.

The more specific you can be in talking to God about what was done to you and how it made you feel, the deeper and more thorough your forgiveness will be. Consider the following two examples of how people might go about trying to forgive:

1. A generic, ineffective way of acknowledging pain and choosing to forgive:
   *Heavenly Father, I know that my Dad hurt me as I was growing up and I guess I've held some things against him. But I forgive him. Amen.*

2. A specific, effective way of acknowledging pain and choosing to forgive:

*Heavenly Father, I have had a lot of anger and resentment toward my Dad because of all the times he called me "loser" or "jerk" or "sissy" or said he wished I'd never been born and that I couldn't do anything right and would never amount to anything. I remember the time he beat the crap out of me so brutally that I had to go to the hospital. I hated him for that. I cried so hard because it hurt so bad, but what really hurt the most was how he rejected me. Other kids had great relationships with their Dads, but I was ashamed of him and all his stupid drinking. Lord, I have felt so much hatred and anger and shame and embarrassment because of him. I have been so afraid and lonely and felt so rejected and helpless. My life would have been way different... so much easier and happier if he hadn't been this way. But now I choose to let go of all my anger and disappointment and embarrassment toward my Dad and I truly forgive him just as You have forgiven me. Amen.*

The difference is obvious. In the first case, the individual is in a hurry, not wanting to truly face the pain that is deep down. It's like he was water skiing, skimming over the suffering in his life, just hurrying to get the prayer over with.

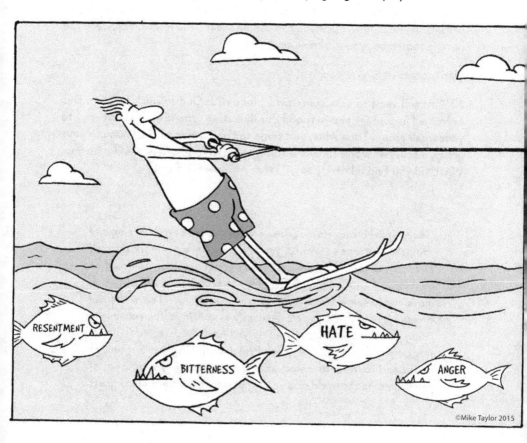

In the second example, the memories were specific, as were the emotional words used. It was like a deep sea diver, going down into the darkness, taking his time, facing what was there with the light of God's grace and truth.

In the first example, there was no real forgiveness extended and no freedom gained. In the second instance, a significant work of God was happening.

### Which will it be for you?

I will conclude with two very simple prayers. They are just models, examples that might help you express what you need to say. For this to be a truly meaningful process for you, however, you're going to have to make *our* prayer *your* prayer. Follow the second example above and be specific in what happened to you and be specific in how those memories affected you emotionally. Getting in touch with the emotional core of your pain is essential to experiencing freedom. That is how you *forgive from the heart.*

Stay with each person on your list until you can't think of anything else to forgive them for; then move on to the next person on the list. And don't be surprised if in the hours, days and weeks ahead you find other memories surfacing. That's okay. God knows how much you can handle today. And if more forgiveness is needed tomorrow, you will know what to do.

Don't forget to forgive yourself.

**≫ You will want to take some time alone with God to work through this exercise. I encourage you to spend this liberating time with the Lord prior to your small group. Then when you come to this portion of the lesson in your group, discuss what this time of working through forgiveness was like for you. What did you find relatively easy? What was more difficult?**

*Finally, if the memories that come to your mind are overwhelming and you need someone to sit with you and pray while you work through this process, talk to the people in your group and see who would do that for you. Going through The Steps to Freedom in Christ (which includes a complete section on forgiveness in Step Three) with a trained encourager could help you tremendously as well. In fact, I recommend going through the "Steps" whether you have deep-seated issues of forgiveness or not. The Steps to Freedom in Christ is a thorough moral and spiritual inventory that has helped many thousands of people around the world resolve their personal and spiritual conflicts.*

Let's begin.

## —— PRAY ——

*Dear heavenly Father, I choose to forgive (name the person) for (be specific in what was done to you) even though it made me feel (be very honest with the emotional pain).*

After you have finished forgiving each person... and assuming that person is still alive...you can pray as follows:

*Father, I choose not to hold any of these things against (name the person) any longer. I declare that Christ's death was sufficient punishment for their sin and so I release any right to revenge. I now ask You to bring great blessing to (name the person). In Jesus' name I pray. Amen.*

May God grant you all the grace you need to work through this process with all the people you need to forgive. Be patient. It may take a while to be thorough, but it is well worth the time and effort. Don't be afraid of the pain or of your emotions. God wants to heal you. This is an important step forward in that direction.

# fighting an invisible war
## KNOW YOUR ENEMY

We know that we have dumped a lot on your plate in the first six studies, and you may be feeling a bit overwhelmed. Hang in there. We're almost done. But before we dive into more stuff and talk about some key issues necessary to getting unstuck, it would be good to briefly review what we have already learned.

As you may recall, in **Study #1** we came up with a definition of "freedom in Christ" and we have been looking at different elements of that freedom ever since. That definition is:

> Freedom in Christ is overcoming sin's power and the devil's lies through repentance and faith in the truth, joyfully living in the fullness of the Holy Spirit as a secure, loved, accepted and significant child of the God of grace.

Though we will never experience this freedom perfectly this side of heaven, the Lord desires that we increasingly live out this lifestyle of liberty. Nothing shall be impossible for God (Luke 1:37). I hope you are already seeing this freedom grow in your life as you complete these studies.

In **Study #2** and **#3** we discussed our *identity in Christ* and our *position in Christ*. We saw that in Him we are indeed *a secure, loved, accepted and significant child of the God of grace*. And we also looked at the truth that we are dead to sin and alive to God in Jesus. Sin is no longer our master, because we are under God's grace not the law. We now have the capacity to *overcome sin's power through repentance*. We are free to use our bodies as instruments of right-living rather than for sin. In Christ our bodies are now the temple of the Holy Spirit.

In **Study #4** we wrestled with the tough issue of why the Christian life can be so hard– understanding how our flesh operates and discovering the freedom of *joyfully living in the fullness of the Holy Spirit*.

**Study #5** and **#6** gave us opportunity to face head-on the tough issues of pain and suffering in life, realizing that a large part of freedom is moving beyond our anger and distrust toward God. We also recognized the very common—though very serious—problem of unresolved anger toward others and ourselves, and the key that unlocks freedom... *forgiveness*.

In these final two studies, we will address the subject of the enemy of our souls, our adversary the devil, so that we can avoid the snares and traps he cunningly places in our paths. First, in **Study #7** we will seek to know the nature and tactics of this enemy... much like a football team diligently watches hours and hours of film of their opponent. Then we will conclude *unstuck* by knowing the weapons God has given us so that, by His grace, we can win this spiritual war. To be victorious, we will need to understand how to walk in freedom from *the devil's lies*, living by *faith in the truth*. That will be the subject of **Study #8**.

Recognizing that the enemies of the Lord Jesus Christ do not want any of their tactics exposed, let's pray for God's protection as we begin:

*Dear heavenly Father, I come before You and worship You as the Holy One, the Majestic One, the Almighty One. Nothing is too difficult for You. You reign as King over the entire universe and I surrender to You now as Lord of all my life. Realizing that the enemy of my soul seeks to steal, kill and destroy (John 10:10), I ask for Your protection from his schemes. Please shine light on all darkness seeking to gain control of my life, for apart from Your supernatural work of revealing his snares and traps, I cannot see them. I thank You that even the darkness is not dark to You; You can see clearly what is hidden as though it were in broad daylight. I pray in the name of Jesus, the Light. Amen.*

The first order of business in this study is to understand our enemy as the Bible reveals him to be. What is his nature, his character? And what are the main tactics that he uses to try and trip us up? Thankfully, God has given us a complete "scouting report."

**»** Before we dive into what the Bible has to say, take a crack at describing the devil yourself. Imagine your job is to alert Christians to Satan... public enemy number one. In the space below, write out your description of the devil. Then take time in your group to tell each other what you came up with.

_____

_____

_____

_____

_____

I really hope your description didn't include any little guys running around in red suits with horns and pitchforks! "Funny" how that caricature has enjoyed such wide publicity in the media. Maybe such a description is designed to make us laugh and not take the devil seriously...? I wonder who might possibly be behind that tactic?

Once again, as I trust you have come to see, there is no place like the Bible when it comes to the bottom line of truth about anything relating to your life in Christ. It includes some great "film" of the enemy that we need to study.

**» Take a look at each of the following Scriptures and underline the things that describe the enemy's character and strategies. Then discuss in your group what you found. Talk about instances when you can look back and realize you were being assaulted by the devil in these ways.**

But one whom you forgive anything, I forgive also; for indeed what I have forgiven, if I have forgiven anything, I did it for your sakes in the presence of Christ, so that no advantage be taken of us by Satan, for we are not ignorant of his schemes.
2 CORINTHIANS 2:10-11

Therefore humble yourselves under the mighty hand of God, that He may exalt you at the proper time, casting all your anxiety on Him, because He cares for you. Be of sober spirit, be on the alert. Your adversary, the devil, prowls around like a roaring lion, seeking someone to devour. But resist him, firm in your faith, knowing that the same experiences of suffering are being accomplished by your brethren who are in the world.
1 PETER 5:6-9

For this reason, when I could endure it no longer, I also sent to find out about your faith, for fear that the tempter might have tempted you, and our labor would be in vain.
1 THESSALONIANS 3:5

Then I heard a loud voice in heaven, saying, "Now the salvation and the power, and the kingdom of our God and the authority of His Christ have come, for the accuser of our brethren has been thrown down, he who accuses them before our God day and night.
REVELATION 12:10

[Jesus speaking to the hard-hearted, unbelieving Pharisees]: You are of your father the devil, and you want to do the desires of your father. He was a murderer from the beginning, and does not stand in the truth because there is no truth in him. Whenever he speaks a lie, he speaks from his own nature, for he is a liar and the father of lies.
JOHN 8:44

*For I am jealous for you with a godly jealousy; for I betrothed you to one husband, so that to Christ I might present you as a pure virgin. But I am afraid that, as the serpent deceived Eve by his craftiness, your minds will be led astray from the simplicity and purity of devotion to Christ... For such men are false apostles, deceitful workers, disguising themselves as apostles of Christ. No wonder, for even Satan disguises himself as an angel of light.*
2 CORINTHIANS 11:2-3, 13-14

In a minute, I'll give you a summary of what those Bible verses have to teach us about the character and tactics of the enemy, but first we need to make a couple of things crystal clear:

- First, the devil is not the "opposite" of God or Christ. God (Father, Son and Holy Spirit) is the eternal Creator of all things; Satan is a created being, as all angels are (see Colossians 1:13-16).

- Second, though the devil is stronger, smarter and faster than we are, neither he nor his demons are even remotely close to being equal with God. Only God is all-powerful. Only God is all-knowing. Only God is everywhere-present (see Psalm 139).

- Third, the devil and his demons must bow to God's authority, and cannot act beyond the boundaries set up by God (see Job 1 and 2; Luke 22:31,32). The devil is on a leash, so to speak.

>> Okay. Let's see how your group did in picking up the main points from the Scriptures listed above. Put a check mark in the chart below next to the ones you and your group members discovered. Circle the ones in the table below that your group hadn't noticed. Then, in your group talk about those new discoveries. Discuss times when you have seen the enemy operate in these ways.

| The nature and activity of Satan | How we stand against him |
|---|---|
| O The devil tries to take advantage of us, especially where there is unresolved conflict, anger and unforgiveness; he is an exploiter, an opportunist. | O Forgive those who have sinned against us or the church; restore to fellowship those who have genuinely repented |
| O Satan employs schemes (cunning strategies) that wage war against our minds. | O Do not be ignorant of his schemes; know how he operates |
| O The devil seeks to overwhelm us with fear and anxiety, seeking to incite us to lose faith and act in our own strength and abilities (apart from God); his intimidation tactics can be as frightening as a lion's roar. | O Live in humility (complete dependence and submission to God); trust Him with your reputation; remember, no matter how tough things get, God cares for you and is caring for you; be sober in spirit; be on the alert; resist the devil's efforts to tempt you to doubt, fear or lose faith/hope in God; remember that you are not alone; others in Christ have suffered and been victorious in Christ. |
| O Satan is, by nature, a tempter and entices us, seeking to lure us into compromise and immorality and to take life into our own hands, meeting our own needs rather than depending on God to meet them. | |
| O The devil continually accuses us of sin, trying to make us feel guilty and shameful; he also tries to incite God against us in order to gain permission to attack us (Luke 22:31) | O Stay close enough to other believers so that there is always someone "watching your back"; make sure there are people around you who will not allow you to withdraw and isolate yourself out of shame, guilt or fear |

○ Satan, by nature, is a liar and he uses lies about God, ourselves, life, etc. in order to keep us under his control; he is a deceiver and can be very subtle; he also is a murderer, and if he could, he would try and kill us.

○ The devil deceives by his craftiness, seeking to lure us away from a simple, pure devotion to Jesus through false religions, New Age and other false teachings, false Christ's, and false teachers; he can even appear as an angel of light, hoping you will listen and obey him.

○ Remember the salvation, power and authority of Christ, through whom all your sins (past, present and future) have been paid for; know that in Christ you are clean!

○ (From John 8:31-36): Make sure you continue reading and studying God's Word and know the truth; knowing the truth will set you free from believing lies that keep you in bondage to sin; Christ Himself is the truth and He will make you free indeed.

○ Stay purely and wholeheartedly devoted to Jesus and do not allow yourself to be led astray by attractive religious ideas or appealing religious figures; see yourself as a pure virgin betrothed to Jesus Christ alone.

There is a lot to chew on in the table above. As you and your fellow group members reflect on your own struggles with the powers of darkness and honestly discuss them together, you can go a long way toward preparing yourself for the spiritual battles that lie ahead. Before we conclude this seventh study, I'd like us to take a look at what could be called the "preamble" to the famous passage on the armor of God (which we will look at in **Study #8**).

*Finally, be strong in the Lord and in the strength of His might. Put on the full armor of God, so that you will be able to stand firm against the schemes of the devil. For our struggle is not against flesh and blood, but against the rulers, against the powers, against the world forces of this darkness, against the spiritual forces of wickedness in the heavenly places. Therefore, take up the full armor of God, so that you will be able to resist in the evil day, and having done everything, to stand firm.*
EPHESIANS 6:10-13

>> There is much to glean from this biblical call to war. Take some time in your group to discuss the following questions: What is the meaning of the first sentence in Ephesians 6:10-13 (Take a stab at putting it into your own words)? According to this passage of Scripture, who is our enemy? How can we be duped into thinking that our primary battle is against people? What is the "evil day" that the writer mentioned (Describe a day that you have had recently when things were so rough you wish you had stayed in bed)? According to Ephesians 6:10-13, what is the objective of fighting spiritual battle?

Here are five points I want to make sure you all picked up:

- **First,** before we are ready to put on the armor of God (listed in Ephesians 6:14-18) we need to make sure we take care of a couple issues. First, we need to be strong in the Lord. Being strong "in the Lord" or strong "in Christ" means knowing who you are in Christ and being secure in that identity. Ephesians chapter one talks all about that. In Christ we are saints; recipients of God's grace and peace; chosen; holy; blameless; adopted as sons; accepted; redeemed; forgiven; lavished with grace; and so on.

  *Do these words describe how you see yourself or are you basing your self-worth and personal security in your appearance, personality, possessions, accomplishments, or financial portfolio?*

  If you know who you are in Christ and are standing on those truths in your daily life, you have a fighting chance of winning spiritual battle. If you aren't, you don't. I know that's blunt, but it's the truth. *Only those who are strong in the Lord... that is, truly living life on the basis of who they are in Christ... can defeat the devil.*

- **Second,** we need to be strong in the strength of His might. The devil will try and trick you into fighting against his tactics of temptation, accusation and deception with your own strength. Jesus didn't even do that, and He was Almighty God on earth! When He went into the desert to be tempted for 40 days by Satan, He went in the power of the Holy Spirit, not in His own strength.

  Spiritual warfare requires spiritual weapons and spiritual (Holy Spirit) strength. Trying to wage war against the enemy by virtue of your own intelligence, eloquence, physical strength, "street smarts", persuasiveness or problem-solving ability is a dead end street. That is, however, exactly what the devil wants you to do. Pride is his "home court advantage." But as you humbly surrender to God and depend on His power and strength and not your own, you snatch that advantage away from him.

- **Third,** we need to put on all the pieces of God's armor in order to resist the enemy. A partial equipping with pieces missing will only lead to dangerous chinks in our armor that the devil will be sure to exploit.

- **Fourth,** no matter how vigorously people oppose us, they are not the real enemy that we are fighting. The powers of darkness are the real enemy. True, the devil can (and often does) use people as his pawns, but if we focus on what other people are doing to us and ignore or neglect the enemy's "behind-the-scenes" tactics, we will lose the battle.

  Therefore, the focus of our warfare needs to be waged in prayer... targeting the invisible powers of darkness which are seeking to manipulate visible people for their purposes. In fact, the Bible says we are to love our enemies and pray for those who persecute us (Luke 6:27). And, as we looked at in the last study, we need to forgive those who hurt us.

- **Fifth,** the objective of this warfare against the attacks of the powers of darkness is to *stand firm* and *resist*. It implies the idea of a piece of ground that you have occupied and which the enemy is seeking to take over... like your body, your mind, your marriage, your kids, your home, your finances and possessions, etc. Though the battle can be very rugged and very ragged, putting on the full armor of God will enable you to stand firm and resist the devil's efforts to take that which does not rightfully belong to him.

*We will look at how to wage and win spiritual war in our eighth and final study. For now, will you join me in prayer?*

## PRAY

*Dear heavenly Father, I have to admit that all this talk about an invisible enemy who hates Christ and isn't all too thrilled about me either is a bit unnerving. I know that I am to be on the alert, but nowhere in the Bible does it say that I should be scared. Well, to be honest, I am kind of scared, so please help me be courageous. I know Your Word says that You have not given me a spirit of fear or timidity but of power, love and a sound mind (2 Timothy 1:7). I recognize, however, my constant need to be completely dependent on You or I will be fair game for being defeated in the evil day of spiritual attack. I can see that this is not child's play but real war. So, with all the sincerity of my heart, I choose to humble myself before You, Lord, and seek my strength in who I am in You and in the mighty power of Your Holy Spirit. Without You, Lord, I'm a doomed victim. With You, Lord, I'm a strong warrior in Christ the Victor. Strengthen my heart and mind for battle, Lord. Please make me a good soldier of Christ Jesus. I begin by first coming fully under Your authority, Jesus. You are my Commander-in-Chief. I belong to you, Lord. Lead me not into temptation, but deliver me from the evil one. For Yours is the kingdom and the power and the glory forever. Amen.*

# winning an invisible war
## KNOW YOUR WEAPONS

In **Study #7** we plunged into the subject of spiritual warfare by taking a look at our enemy, the devil. He is a formidable foe but has already been defeated by Christ's work on the cross. Knowing that Christ has already won the war will give you strength to persevere and win the battles in life. Looking at a few Scriptures that declare Christ as Victor is a great way to encourage our hearts as we begin.

>> After each Scripture below, write a one or two sentence summary of what
that verse(s) is saying. Take a few minutes in your group to talk about how
these truths provide encouragement for you, and then pray for each other
that these truths would become powerfully real to you.

*Therefore, since the children share in flesh and blood, He Himself [Christ]
likewise also partook of the same, that through death He might render
powerless him who had the power of death, that is, the devil, and might
free those who through fear of death were subject to slavery all their lives.*
HEBREWS 2:14-15 *[word in bracket is mine]*

MY SUMMARY:

_____

_____

_____

_____

_____

*When He [Christ] had disarmed the rulers and authorities [spiritual powers
of darkness], He made a public display of them, having triumphed over them
through the cross.*
COLOSSIANS 2:15 *[words in brackets are mine]*

MY SUMMARY:

_____

_____

_____

_____

_____

> *...and what is the surpassing greatness of His power toward us who believe. These are in accordance with the working of the strength of His might which He brought about in Christ when He raised Him from the dead and seated Him at His right hand in the heavenly places, far above all rule and authority and power and dominion, and every name that is named, not only in this age but also in the one to come. And He put all things in subjection under His feet, and gave Him as head over all things to the church, which is His body, the fullness of Him who fills all in all."*
> EPHESIANS 1:19-23

## MY SUMMARY:

_____

_____

_____

_____

_____

Jesus has come to destroy (undo) the devil's works (1 John 3:8) and greater is He that is in you (the Spirit of Christ) than he that is in the world (the spirit of Antichrist, which is Satan) (1 John 4:4). You and I are on the winning side! We are not waging war for the purpose of trying to win the ultimate victory; we are waging war knowing that victory is already ours in Christ. In fact, we have already been raised up with Christ and seated at God's right hand (see Ephesians 2:6). That is the place of Christ's authority over all the powers of darkness. In Christ, the Church is ultimate victor, because Christ is Victor. We have read the last chapter of the Book. We win! Let that truth remain in the forefront of your mind when life's daily battles are hard.

The devil, by the way, knows he is a defeated foe and he knows his time left to operate is short and so he is furiously seeking to do as much damage as possible before his end comes (see Revelation 12:12). So how do we enter into Christ's victory and defeat the powers of darkness that seek to oppress us? *That is the subject of this eighth and final study.*

If Christ is the *head* and the Church is His *body*, then the powers of darkness are under the authority of Christ exercised through His Church, right? If that is the case, shouldn't there be a lot more victories for the kingdom of God in the world than are currently happening? What's wrong?

The problem is that we (the body of Christ) are often rendered powerless to exercise that authority because we have been deceived. We end up being too busy with other things of this material world; too prayerless; too compromising with evil; and too divided among ourselves to fight the real battles... against the devil! Tragically, too often we end up fighting a losing battle against sin and a terribly misguided battle against each other rather than waging a winning war against Satan!

>> Take a moment in your group and discuss that last paragraph. What do you see happening in the Church (the body of Christ) that you know has to hamper our ability to defeat Satan? What are the sins of the Church that rob us of our spiritual authority and give the devil free reign to do what he wants? If needed, go ahead and confess any part you personally have played or are currently playing in this problem.

Though we cannot change the entire body of Christ, we can pray for her (the Church), seek to bring unity (e.g. When was the last time your church reached out to serve and bless another congregation?), and we can live in such a way as to defeat the enemy's attacks against us personally. We have the authority to do that, but first we must meet a couple requirements:

## STANDING UNDER

The spiritual world operates under authority. God has instituted that system and all the angels–both good and evil–understand it. It is only we humans that seem to be slow to "get it." One man that Jesus marveled at understood it very well. This man was a centurion, a Roman soldier responsible for 100 men, and his servant was desperately sick. The soldier sent word to Jesus through some Jewish elders, asking the Lord to heal him. Jesus was on his way to do just that when the centurion sent word again. Watch what he says to Jesus and then watch Jesus' reaction to what he said:

*Lord, do not trouble Yourself further, for I am not worthy for You to come under my roof; for this reason I did not even consider myself worthy to come to You, but just say the word, and my servant will be healed. For I also am a man placed under authority, with soldiers under me; and I say to this one, "Go!" and he goes, and to another, "Come!" and he comes, and to my slave, "Do this!" and he does it. Now when Jesus heard this, He marveled at him, and turned and said to the crowd that was following Him, "I say to you, not even in Israel have I found such great faith".*

LUKE 7:6B-9

**》 In your group, discuss this question: What was it about the centurion's faith that impressed Jesus so much?**

There are two reasons, it seems, that Jesus marveled at the centurion's faith – the first reason being fairly obvious, the second being a bit more subtle. The first reason was that the man recognized Jesus' authority to heal by His word, not by His presence (or touch) alone. Therefore, Jesus could have been anywhere, given the command for healing and it would have happened. That's a pretty amazing insight for a non-Jew in that day to have!

The second reason is tucked away in the soldier's statement, *"For I also am a man placed under authority..."* Most of us would probably have said something like, "For I also am a man *with* authority." But that's not what the centurion said. He recognized that Jesus, like himself, was *under* authority! The centurion was right. Jesus never did anything on His own initiative but only what God the Father was telling Him and showing Him to do (see John 5:19,20). Jesus, even though He was, is, and always will be God, while on earth acted in complete submission to God the Father!

Here is an extremely important spiritual principle:

> *You can only exercise authority in the spiritual realm when you are under authority.*

**》 If you are a normal human being, you may be squirming a little bit here. Let's face it, most of us don't like being under authority because we don't like other people telling us what to do. We think we know better and we chafe against anything that "cramps our style". What is your gut level reaction to the word "submission"? Have a heart-to-heart talk about that question in your group.**

There is great danger in rebellion and great safety in submission to the authorities God has placed in our lives. That's why James 4:6-7 teaches:

> *But He gives a greater grace. Therefore it says, "God is opposed to the proud, but gives grace to the humble." Submit therefore to God. Resist the devil and he will flee from you.*
>
> JAMES 4:6-7

Do you see the progression? It is plain and simple. First, humbly submit to God's authority and any human authorities He has placed in your life. Second, resist the devil. If you are truly submitting to God, then and only then, will you have the spiritual authority to resist the devil. If you are not living your life under submission to God's rule, His Lordship, you can try and resist the devil until you are blue in the face but it won't work. The only times we are permitted by God to not submit to human authority are when those authorities are seeking to make us do that which God forbids or are trying to hinder us from doing what God commands (see Acts 4:18-20).

**» Ask God to show you how completely you are humbly submitting to His Lordship in your life. How are you doing in submitting to the laws of the land, including tax and traffic laws? Your employer? Your spouse? Church leaders? (If a minor or student) Your parents or teachers or coaches? In your group, use the prayer below to confess honestly any specific ways that you are rebelling against God or the authorities He has placed in your life. Remember that a rebellious spirit can be at work in our hearts, even if outwardly we are pretending to submit. Don't forget: What you say and pray in your group, stays in your group.**

## ── PRAY ──

*Dear heavenly Father, I have to admit that at times I have had a rebellious heart and a non-submissive spirit toward You and the authorities You have placed in my life. Specifically, I have sinned by (mention specific ways you have rebelled in your heart and/or in actions). I thank You for shining the light of Your truth on this area and I choose now to adopt a submissive spirit and a servant's heart. I can only do this by the power of Your Spirit, so please fill me with the Holy Spirit. Thank You for Your forgiveness. In Jesus' name I pray, amen.*

## STANDING FIRM

Last week we looked at the "preamble" to the great "armor of God" passage of Ephesians 6. That Scripture makes it clear that unless you are walking in the security that comes from knowing your identity in Christ and unless you are leaning on God's power rather than your own, you're already defeated when it comes to spiritual warfare. But for those who are "strong in the Lord and in the strength of His might", there are mighty weapons of warfare that God has given us to fight and win spiritual battle. These weapons are known as "the armor of God."

Before examining the armor of God, you need to realize something very important, and the reason I have to mention it is because of a problem with the English language. When we see the word "you" written or implied, we tend to think "me", that is, "you singular." Our rugged, frontier individualism here in the West contributes to that perception. But the "you" implied in Ephesians 6:10-18 is not singular, but plural. It is a call to the church to lock arms and armor together to wage victorious warfare in community, not in isolation. In fact, isolation is one of the enemy's most effective tactics against us. It's not just you against the devil. It's us against the powers of darkness... together.

©Mike Taylor 2015

And the purpose is to stand firm. When the smoke clears and the dust settles on the spiritual battlefield, God wants us to be standing strong. And He has made a way for us to do just that: *The Armor of God.*

**First,** Ephesians 6:14 says,

> *"Stand firm therefore, having girded your loins with truth..."*

A Roman soldier would wear a belt or girdle around his waist. It did more than keep his pants up. (Okay, just kidding. They didn't wear pants in those days). It was essential for strength and support in battle.

**» Why do you think having a firm handle on God's truth is so important for spiritual battle? Is there a reason this piece of armor is mentioned first? What does truth guard you from? Discuss these questions in your group.**

Satan is called a liar and the father of lies (John 8:44) and lying and deceiving are his greatest weapons. He tries to make us believe what is evil is actually good and vice versa. He slanders God's good character, trying to paint a picture of Him that He is distant, disinterested, uninvolved or uncaring, angry or abusive. Therefore, it is essential that we know the truth. Knowing the truth of the word of God and knowing the Truth, Jesus Himself, will set us free.

---

*Your word I have treasured in my heart, that I may not sin against You.*
PSALM 119:11

---

How full is your heart's "treasure chest" with God's truth? Are you filling your mind with God-things or do you open the door to that which brings compromise or corruption? On the next few pages I want to introduce you to the "Philippians 4:8 Filter"... a project that uses Philippians 4:8 as a guide to determine the things you should think about or not think about.

Here is that verse:

---

*Finally, brethren, whatever is true, whatever is honorable, whatever is right, whatever is pure, whatever is lovely, whatever is of good repute, if there is any excellence and if anything worthy of praise, dwell on these things.*
PHILIPPIANS 4:8

---

One of the enemy's names is the "god of this world" (2 Corinthians 4:4). And 1 John 5:19 says that *"the whole world lies in the power of the evil one."* Basically, Satan has a strong grip on culture, including American culture, and his values are constantly being injected into and advertised through the media. The devil has a very well-designed propaganda strategy to influence our minds away from what is true, honorable, right, pure, etc.

≫ Fill out the following two lists as a means of seeing what kinds of messages you are allowing into your mind. Ask God to give you His perspective about the movies (theater, DVD, online), books, magazines, music, Internet websites, TV shows, commercials, computer and video games, etc. that you are allowing yourself to be exposed to. Put them into the appropriate category below based on what the Lord shows you. I've included an example.

You will notice that we are not giving you the FICM list of "the good, the bad and the ugly" media. First, it would be outdated before we even went to print. Second, it would become a legalistic list of our opinions. It's much better to allow the Holy Spirit... in real time... to show you what He thinks of your media influences. So ask Him to show you and trust that He will.

## PHILIPPIANS 4:8 FILTER
### healthy input I'm allowing into my mind

### true
ex. reading *My Utmost for His Highest* daily

_____

_____

_____

_____

### honorable

_____

_____

_____

_____

### right

_____

_____

_____

_____

### pure

_____

_____

_____

_____

lovely

_____

_____

_____

_____

of good reputation

_____

_____

_____

_____

excellence

_____

_____

_____

_____

worthy of praise

_____

_____

_____

_____

## OPPOSITE OF PHILIPPIANS 4:8
### unhealthy input I'm allowing into my mind

### false (deceptive)

ex. reading the *Book of Mormon*

### Immoral (dishonorable)

### Wrong (unbiblical)

### Impure (provoking lust)

Gruesome (grotesque, cruel)

_____

_____

_____

_____

Of bad, evil reputation

_____

_____

_____

_____

Poor quality (wasteful of time & energy)

_____

_____

_____

_____

Worthy of rebuke and avoidance

_____

_____

_____

_____

» **This exercise will be even more helpful for you if you discuss some of your findings (in both categories) with your group. Tell the others which things are hardest for you to give up. Pray for one another.**

If you want to fully put on the first piece of armor, you will need to decide to embrace those things in the first list and remove those things from the second list from your life. By so doing you'll be going a long way toward "having girded your loins with truth" (Ephesians 6:14).

**Second,** Ephesians 6:14 says,

> *...having put on the breastplate of righteousness.*

This piece of armor involves at least these things:

- Realize that in *Christ* you are already forgiven of all sin, past, present and future (Ephesians 1:7; Colossians 1:13,14; Colossians 2:13,14; Hebrews 10:17,18)

- In *Christ* you are already the righteousness of God (2 Corinthians 5:21).

- When you do sin, confess it promptly and claim God's forgiveness and cleansing (see 1 John 1:9). Don't let the accuser fire his darts of guilt and shame into your mind. "There is therefore now no condemnation for those in Christ Jesus" (Romans 8:1 ESV).

- You have the responsibility to follow Romans 13:12-14 which says, "The night is almost gone, and the day is near. Therefore let us lay aside the deeds of darkness and put on the armor of light. Let us behave properly as in the day, not in carousing and drunkenness, not in sexual promiscuity and sensuality, not in strife and jealousy. But put on the Lord Jesus Christ, and make no provision for the flesh in regard to its lusts."

» **Here is another very valuable place to stop for a few minutes and talk with your group. Discuss together these questions: In what ways are you making yourself vulnerable to temptation because you are "making provision" for fleshly lusts? In other words, how do you plan ahead to sin by the places you choose to go, the things you purchase, the times you wait to make sure you are alone, etc.?**

As you are talking honestly with one another, pray for each other and commit yourselves to continue to pray for and help one another overcome these threats to freedom. This is where the rubber meets the road in terms of personal holiness and morality. We hope by this time you have found such an atmosphere of trust and freedom in your small group that you can be honest. When you tell the truth, there is hope for healing; when you hide your sin, there is none.

---

*He who conceals his transgressions will not prosper, but he who confesses and forsakes them will find compassion.*
PROVERBS 28:13

---

**Third,** Ephesians 6:15 says,

*and having shod your feet with the preparation of the gospel of peace;*

Again, this piece of armor has several components to it:

- Know that you are at peace with God through your faith in our Lord Jesus Christ (Romans 5:1).
- Experience peace (the antidote to the devil's attacks of fear and anxiety) by choosing *not* to worry, but instead casting all cares on the Lord in prayer, thanking Him for being in control (Philippians 4:6,7; 1 Peter 5:7).
- Being a peacemaker by always being ready to bring the good news of salvation to those around you (Matthew 5:9; 1 Peter 3:15).

**≫ What have you been worried about? What are the anxieties that dominate your thinking and keep you awake at night? What fears or worries do you need to cast onto the broad shoulders of Jesus today? Take a moment before moving on to pray and present each of those anxieties to Him. If you don't, they can become crushing burdens to you. Imagine that you are hoisting them off your shoulders and placing them onto His. He can handle them; you can't.**

**If you have time, tell others in your group about the burdens you have carried and ask them to pray for you. That will help you seal the deal of letting them go, and not taking them back. God really does care for you and can be trusted with anything and everything in your life.**

The first three elements of the Christian soldier's armor are meant to always be in place. It is never safe to take off the armor of God. When the battle gets heavy in or around you that is not the time to try and put on the first three pieces. You need to be walking in truth, righteousness and peace as a way of life.

There are times, however, when the enemy plays really rough and you can feel like you are right in his crosshairs. The Bible calls that "the evil day." When the devil strikes with particularly vicious attacks, you will also need the last three pieces. Before we look at those last three pieces, circle any of the situations listed below that you are going through right now.

| | | |
|---|---|---|
| Deep grief over loss of a loved one | A child who is rebellious or a runaway | Chronic illness or disability yourself |
| Chronic pain or illness in a loved one | Serious financial distress or acute debt | A child who is depressed or suicidal |
| Loss of a job | Acute physical pain | Slander of your reputation |
| Rejection from family members | Unfair criticism at work or church | Loss of property due to fire or accident |
| Threats against your life or loved one | Strong persecution for your faith | Criminal activity against your property |

| Irrational terror (especially at night) | Depression, loneliness, chronic anxiety | Marital conflict, separation or divorce |
|---|---|---|
| A moral failure | Division or split at church | Debilitating physical injury |

**»** In your group, take a few minutes now and let the other members know what you circled in the lists above. If you feel comfortable and time allows, tell the story of what you are going through. Then take some time together in prayer to ask for God's protection, wisdom, strength and deliverance in these times of trial. Make any notes in the space below of what the Lord reveals to you through the prayers of your brothers/sisters in Christ. This is not the time for isolation. It is the time for a band of brothers or sisters or a group of friends to pull together and stick together.

_____

_____

_____

_____

_____

When life plays hardball with us, we desperately need to cling to Christ even as the enemy seems to assail us with all his hellish weapons. He will try and do everything he can to discourage us. Fortunately, God has given us His weapons, His armor that is stronger than anything the enemy can throw at us. We will conclude with Ephesians 6:16-18, some words of explanation and a final prayer.

_... in addition to all, taking up the shield of faith with which you will be able to extinguish all the flaming arrows of the evil one. And take the helmet of salvation and the sword of the Spirit, which is the word of God. With all prayer and petition pray at all times in the Spirit, and with this in view, be on the alert with all perseverance and petition for all the saints._
EPHESIANS 6:16-18

Here are some important points to make sure you grasp from that Scripture:

- Regardless of what fiery arrows the enemy shoots, you can live by faith and not fear. Knowing that the God who loves you and won't let you go is in control and that nothing can take you from His hand (Romans 8:36-39; John 10:27-30) will enable you to walk by faith. This is the shield of faith. You can know the assurance that King David had: "Lo, though I walk through the valley of the shadow of death, I fear no evil for Thou art with me" (Psalm 23:4).

  *The shield of faith... yours and those of your brothers and sisters around you... is invincible!*

- Knowing that you are saved and safe and secure with the everlasting arms of God underneath you (Deuteronomy 33:27), even if you experience great loss—even death—you can remain sane and full of peace with God's helmet of salvation protecting your mind. This piece of armor is what has enabled saints throughout history to die victoriously as martyrs for their faith in Christ. It is also what has enabled even more saints throughout history to go through daily suffering without losing their minds.

  *The helmet of the hope of salvation (1 Thessalonians 5:8) will marvelously guard your mind against the worst this world and the devil himself throw at you!*

- When the enemy hurls His temptations, accusations and lies at you, don't just stand there, defend yourself! Speak truth from the word of God (applicable to that situation) out loud to him (since he cannot read your mind). Jesus did that in Matthew 4 and defeated the enemy simply by the word of God spoken in the power of the Holy Spirit! That is your sword. Know it well! Use it skillfully!

  *Though most of God's armor is defensive, the sword of the Spirit is offensive. It sings with the power of God and makes the enemy tremble and run when wielded by a saint who knows his or her identity, position and authority in Christ!*

- Rally the troops to pray for you. Don't try to win the battle alone. As we pray fervently and continuously for one another, we become an invincible army!

I ran across this quote recently from A.C. Dixon, 19th Century pastor:

*"When we rely upon organization, we get what organization can do; when we rely upon education, we get what education can do; when we rely upon eloquence, we get what eloquence can do. But when we rely upon prayer, we get what God can do."*

*— A.C. Dixon*

We encourage you to learn to protect your mind by "taking every thought captive to the obedience of Christ" (2 Corinthians 10:5). As you guard your mind with the "Philippians 4:8 Filter" and seek to pour truthful, biblical input into your thought life, when a negative or untrue thought tries to invade, you will recognize it as false. And you are far less likely to let it in. Turn your thoughts to the truth of Scripture or begin to praise and worship God and you will keep that intrusive lie-thought out!

**Let's finish this study in prayer.**

## PRAY

*Dear heavenly Father, I thank You for the armor that You have given me. As I walk humbly before You and stand under Your authority, I can put on the full armor of God and stand firm against the schemes of the evil one. Continue to train me for battle, Lord, and bring around me strong soldiers of Jesus so that together we can resist the enemy and glorify Your holy name. Thank You for these eight studies on freedom. I know I'm just a beginner, but I welcome Your continued guidance as I walk each day of my life along this journey to freedom. In Jesus' powerful, truthful, loving, liberating name I pray, amen.*

©Mike Taylor 2015

This study wraps up *unstuck*, but we sincerely hope it has only served to whet your appetite for more study, learning and growth in your journey into freedom. In fact, if you would like to dig deeper into this crucial subject of freedom in Christ, we encourage you to pick up a copy of *Journey to Freedom* available online at freedominchrist.com.

In addition, if you have never gone through *The Steps to Freedom in Christ* by Dr. Neil T. Anderson, we heartily encourage you to do so. That booklet is also available at freedominchrist.com. Going through the "Steps" can be one of the most liberating and transformational experiences of your entire life and could very well pave the way for you to move powerfully ahead into greater freedom and maturity in Christ.

To contact Freedom in Christ Ministries, you can email us at info@ficm.org
Or call us toll-free at 1-866-462-4747

# And make sure you get all three studies in "the unusual series":

### unstuck: free from

Most Christians are stuck and don't know how to get free. In these eight heart-transforming studies, you will tackle the big obstacles to growth in Christ and discover God's powerful liberating truths for your life.

### undaunted: free to

Once we have experienced freedom in Christ, we can live life courageously in the power of the Spirit. Learn how freedom is the gateway to fruitful ministry in... prayer, worship, evangelism, humanitarian service, standing against injustice and more!

### unearthed: free forever

Your future hope and freedom gives you strength to endure present trials. This book will help get you really ready for all the world may throw at you in the days to come. Find out how to be a catalyst to spreading that hope to others, no matter what lies ahead.

# NOTES

CPSIA information can be obtained
at www.ICGtesting.com
Printed in the USA
BVHW091649161221
624206BV00010B/804

9 780996 972512